LONG story SHORT

LONG story SHORT

GOD, ETERNITY, HISTORY AND YOU

JOHN KITCHEN

CLC

PUBLICATIONS

Fort Washington, PA 19034

Published by CLC Publications

U.S.A.
P.O. Box 1449, Fort Washington, PA 19034

GREAT BRITAIN
51 The Dean, Alresford, Hants SO24 9BJ

AUSTRALIA
P.O. Box 469, Kippa-Ring QLD 4021

NEW ZEALAND
118 King Street, Palmerston North 4410

Printed in the United States of America
18 17 16 15 14 13 12 11 10   1 2 3 4 5 6

ISBN-13 (trade paper): 978-1-936143-08-5

Dedicated to

Melody, Joe and Clint

May God make you glad captives to His story—
may you thus discover your own.

Contents

Acknowledgments

I was not raised in the church. I didn't begin attending Sunday school until I was in my senior year of high school. So I had a lot of catching up to do the next year when I landed in a Bible college! Everyone seemed far ahead of me. But over the course of my studies, God enabled me to learn a great deal about the Bible. I was, however, still missing something . . . and I knew it. This was not the failure of the college, but was a natural part of my progression in discipleship.

I had data. Not perfectly, but fairly comprehensively. I possessed facts, but I did not yet see—at least not as I wished to. There was much more for me to learn (isn't there always!), but more than anything, I needed illumination. I needed sight! I needed to see what I had learned.

I recall telling my wife, "I have the data. I can line up the biblical characters and events in chronological order. But I can't picture it all. I can't see the big picture, the plan, the unfolding of how it all fits together!" This hunger turned into a prayer, a prayer that God answered through a man named James M. "Buck" Hatch. I never actually met Mr. Hatch, though we hustled about the same campus. But I sat under his teaching—via cassette tape (now I am dating myself!)—in a course called The Progress of Redemption.[1] During those hours of lecture, reading and study, God did a miracle—He began to open my eyes. I began to see, from the Scriptures, God's great plan for the ages. God illuminated my heart with a vision of His glory.

That was well over twenty years ago, and Mr. Hatch is now

in the Lord's presence. I have gone on to read much else since then. I've done further study on my own. But it was in those days and through Mr. Hatch's instruction that God opened my eyes for the first time to see what it is He is doing in all of history.

What I write here is not a rehash of Mr. Hatch's material, though it is built upon the foundation he laid in my life and the lives of many others. Any mistakes, errors or failures are mine alone. My prayer, however, is that God would use this little volume to give to you the gift He gave to me years ago—the chance to see the big thing God is doing in all of history. There is nothing more compelling than a heaven-sent view of God's glory and how He is working toward its full revelation. Nothing is more life altering than to see your life in the light of God's purpose.

I wish to express my thanks to the great folks at CLC Publications. Their trust is a wonderful gift. I express my appreciation to Becky English, my editor. Her skill in balancing the overall vision for this project and the necessary attention to detail made this a far better book.

I thank my dear wife, Julie. Her patience with me—not merely as a writer, but also as her husband—is astounding and life transforming. Thanks go also to our children Melody, Joe and Clint. You bring me such joy. I love you all!

Then, also, the entire message of this book would be contradicted if I did not seek to express my greatest thanks to the God of all glory for His unspeakable grace invested in my life. *Sola gratia. Soli Deo gloria!*

INTRODUCTION

Tell Me a Story

Tell me a story.
    In this century, and moment of mania,
Tell me a story.
    Make it a story of great distances, and starlight.
The name of the story will be Time,
    But you must not pronounce its name.
Tell me a story of deep delight.

                    —Robert Penn Warren

Sadly, when many people hear or see the word "story," they think only of fiction. Their minds race back to childhood nursery rhymes or bedtime stories, calling up images of make-believe characters in contrived lands facing made-up challenges. It is significant, I think, that Webster first defines the word "story" as "a statement regarding the *facts* pertinent to a situation in question" before it offers the option of "a fictional narrative."[1]

I recall the way things unfolded in our home. When our children were small, after they had brushed their teeth and been snuggly tucked under cozy covers each evening, bedtime always elicited the repeated request, "Will you tell me a story?" My response was just as predictable: "Real or pretend?" The answer "Real!" was a call for something that had actually happened and which had direct correspondence to actual events. It called for a good memory on my part. The reply "Pretend!" called for inventiveness. Accuracy was not the point of such yarns; creativity was.

11

When we speak of the Bible as *story* or *narrative*, it is my children's former answer rather than their latter that applies. I unabashedly and unashamedly contend that the stories in the Bible and the story *of* the Bible are true. They are accurate as to the facts. As Peter asserts, they are not "cleverly invented stories" (2 Pet. 1:16). They are, rather, history.

Eventually, the old adage "History is His story" will prove to be a trustworthy perspective on the events of time and space. God's story is unfolded before us in the pages of Scripture—through media such as historical books, poetic prayers, prophetic oracles and instructional epistles. Some folks will tell you that truth is stranger than fiction. I suppose that may be true, but I believe it is more accurate to say that truth is more dramatic than fiction. Drama does not dwell solely in the territory of fiction. I think it is fair to suggest that fiction does not offer nearly the dramatic power that fact does.

Thus, taking the scriptural record as reliable history, I ask you also to see it as an unfolding drama—not fiction, but drama. When you are willing to let yourself see it as such, I believe the story will grip your heart and will soon begin to direct your steps. As the wonder of His story begins to envelop you, a fresh understanding of your own story will also begin to emerge. Direction will become clearer. Confidence to step forward will well up. Courage for the path ahead will swell within you. Your story will have found a context that gives it meaning, purpose, significance and hope. Such is the power of His story.

The closing chapter of the final installment of C.S. Lewis's *Chronicles of Narnia* is entitled "Farewell to Shadowlands." As the *Chronicles* draw to a close, Aslan the lion—the Christ figure throughout the saga—speaks to Peter, Susan, Edmund and Lucy one final time. Lewis draws the parting picture for us:

> And as He spoke, He no longer looked to them like a lion; but the things that began to happen after that were so great

and beautiful that I cannot write them. And for us this is the end of all the stories. . . . But for them it was only the beginning of the real story. All their life in this world and all their adventures in Narnia had only been the cover and the title page: now at last they were beginning Chapter One of the Great Story which no one on earth has read: which goes on for ever: in which every chapter is better than the one before.[2]

My hope for the pages that lie ahead is that they might enable you to live your story now in light of the unfolding, eternal story of God—which will prove to have been the real story all along. My prayer is that one day, as you step into God's presence, you will discover that the story you've lived during your puff of time on this earth has been woven seamlessly into the story He has been unfolding from the beginning and will continue wondrously to unfold for all eternity.

PART 1

HISTORY

History never looks like history when you are living through it. It always looks
confusing and messy, and it always feels uncomfortable.
—**John W. Gardner**

History is a vast early warning system.
—**Norman Cousins**

History is a guide to navigation in perilous times.
—**David C. McCullough**

History is the witness that testifies to the passing of time; it illumines reality,
vitalizes memory, provides guidance in daily life and brings us tidings of antiquity.
—**Cicero**

The Master Plan

Tell Me the Real *Story*

I still recall the ringing of the phone and my rising to answer it, though it was almost twenty years ago. It was a rare event to have an evening at home alone, so I wasn't thrilled to hear the phone ring. As I picked up the receiver, I heard a voice I did not recognize greeting me in an enthusiastic and friendly tone, saying, "How's it going?" "Fine," I replied, trying desperately to filter the sound through the voice-recognition system in my head. I wasn't getting any hits, so I tried to buy time: "How are *you* doing?" "Fine," came the reply. And so the conversation rolled on—me completely lost as to whom I was speaking with, the other person completely certain of who he had reached.

Eventually, however, I began picking up on some clues that told me I wasn't who he thought I was. So I started asking some probing questions. The other person thought it was a joke. I pressed further. He got irritated and told me to stop playing games with him. And on it went.

Finally, I convinced him that he had the wrong person. I managed to extract from him that he was calling from California and was seeking someone in a different part of the country whose area code was only slightly different from ours. After a closing exchange of comments in which he said things like "Oh, I'm sorry" and "Guess that's kind of embarrassing!" we hung up.

Over the years I've thought a number of times about that

conversation, wondering, what would it be like if we lived our entire lives inside a conversation like that? What I mean is this: What if you and I lived our entire lives thinking we were in a different conversation than the one that is really going on? What if we lived out our lives in a drama that appears to be unfolding—only to discover that the part we thought we played was never really written into the *actual* story in fact being written? What if our assumptions about what is really going on in this world are all wrong and we live our lives off-purpose?

Could there be anything more important than knowing we've got the real story straight in our understanding? Is there anything more essential than knowing what purposes are being worked out in the unfolding of history? If we fail in this, we may well get to the end of our days and discover we've wasted the one life we've been given. And worse, we might find we're being held responsible for what we've done with that life!

What's the Real Story?

For these reasons I am extending an invitation to you. It is an invitation to look again at God's story with the anticipation that when you do, you'll be enabled to discover the story God wants to make of your unique and individual life.

But, to be fair, some believe such a discovery to be impossible. It is unattainable, they contend, because no such grand plan exists—there is no overarching purpose to discover. Therefore, without any master plan, there can be no personal purpose.

So, we need to ask, Is there one grand, overarching story to all of history? Is there one cohesive story being written across the scroll of history? Many believe that history is simply random fragments of billions of smaller, personal stories that people are trying to write with the pen of their choices and the ink of their sweat and blood. They say there is not one, big, overarching story, and that we live in a world of chaos, without rhyme or reason.

The renowned British historian G.N. Clark, in his inaugural address at Cambridge University, said, "There is no secret and no plan in history to be discovered." André Maurois, the French biographer, critic and novelist said, "The universe is indifferent. Who created it? Why are we here on this puny mud heap spinning in infinite space? I have not the slightest idea and I am convinced no one has."[1]

Such an understanding leaves us with an ethic that cries, in the words of the ancient Scripture, "Let us eat and drink, for tomorrow we die!" (Isa. 22:13, NKJV; see also 1 Cor. 15:32). If there is no grand story being written, then there is no point to any of the individual acts that take place in this world. If there is no point, there is no purpose. If there is no purpose, there is no morality. There is no right or wrong, there is just now. And the wisest thing I can do, under such a worldview, is to please my glands and impulses as fully as possible in this instant. In such a world there is no morality. But, if we are honest, neither can there be any hope.

I'm telling you today, *that* world does not exist. That "conversation"—in which most of our world is engaged at this moment—is the result of a wrong number. Living in an unreal scenario means wasting one's life, for it ignores an approaching appointment already on the books.

My invitation is this: Come with me back to the beginning and begin a journey which will deliver us at the end. I want you to see from Scripture that there is one grand story, one true story that is being written across history, and that your life can be a part of it. Your life can contribute to the fulfillment and completion of that story. You are not an accident. The ordering of your life is not a mistake. There is a point to it all and a purpose for your existence. Your life can have meaning and can contribute to what God is doing from all eternity.

We are, in one sense, going to travel the Bible from cover to cover—from Genesis to Revelation. But we aren't just going to say, "This is the book of Genesis. Here is what is talked about in Genesis. And here is the book of Galatians. Here is who wrote Galatians." That is data—important data, to be sure! But we need more than just information; we need insight. We need more than just to *know*; we need to *see*! My prayer is that you will *see* the story that the data traces. I want you to *see* the unfolding drama of what God has been doing from eternity past and which He will complete in eternity future.

The Bible is the inspired Word of God. It is "God-breathed" (2 Tim. 3:16). Its words are the very exhale of God. That applies at every level—words, sentences, paragraphs, chapters (though the chapter breaks are not inspired), books and even testaments. God breathed meaning into every layer of the Scriptures.

To illustrate, let me ask you, what do you think of when I use the word "orbit"? You likely know that there are orbits going on at the atomic level—as electrons whirl around the nucleus of the atom. You know that there is an orbit of the moon around our planet. You know that our planet and its co-planets orbit around the sun, making up our solar system. Did you know that our solar system moves with all the other solar systems that make up our galaxy, revolving around a core? At every level we find consistent, purposeful movement going on.

In this study we are going to look for the big movement of God throughout His written story. We are not going to dig much into the minutiae of words and sentences. Rather, we will be looking for the Holy Spirit–inspired movements taking place across the whole backdrop of history as recounted in the Bible. By this approach we'll find ourselves often wishing we could stop and unpack some of the details along the way. But we will largely resist that urge. We'll do so because my hope is that, after you have seen the big picture, you'll be able to read your Bible more knowledgeably, putting the detail in its proper context.

Not an Eternal Left Turn!

Just because I used orbits as an illustration, don't conclude that history is cyclical. History is not cyclical but linear. There are those who claim that things just move in circles—that what has been will be and what is has already been. They'll tell you there is no meaning, no significant movement toward a climactic purpose. History, some assert, is like the stairs on an escalator that circle endlessly around, always moving but never really arriving anywhere. The fact is, however, that history moves in a straight line to an appointed destination.

This is just what we find in the Scriptures: Paul can write of God's "eternal purpose" (Eph. 3:11). He can affirm that God "works out everything in conformity with the purpose of his will" (1:11). God says, "I make known the end from the beginning, from ancient times, what is still to come. I say: My purpose will stand, and I will do all that I please" (Isa. 46:10). That is why He is rightly called "the King of the ages" (1 Tim. 1:17, esv). Paul accurately declared that "known to God from eternity are all His works" (Acts 15:18, nkjv). The writer of Hebrews tells us that in all this, "God wanted to make the unchanging nature of his purpose very clear" (Heb. 6:17). That is what I am hoping will happen during our journey—that God's unchanging purpose will become very clear.

Preparing for the Journey

God wants you to know this grand story, His story. And He wants you to discover your part in it. In just a moment we are going to launch out. But I don't want us to embark empty handed. I'm first going to provide you an essential travel tip. This will prove priceless; keep this knowledge ever near during your journey. The success of your trek will depend upon it.

Are you ready? There are two things which will always help you find your way in this story. If at any point in our journey you think you've lost your way and if none of it is making any sense, you must bring these two unchangeable constants into view. With them you will always be able to gain your bearings, no matter where you find yourself in this journey from eternity past to eternity future.

Ancient mariners used an instrument called a sextant, an ingenious device that operates at all times from two fixed points. To use it properly, you must sight in both the sun (or the moon or a star) and the horizon. Using those fixed points, you are able, with amazing accuracy, to judge your travel and to progress toward your destination. If you know how to use the sextant and can locate those two points, you will never truly be lost.

OK, no more suspense. Here are the two fixed points you'll need to constantly remember, and which will always be visible in our race from eternity past to eternity future, no matter where you may find yourself. Ready? Here they are: *glory* and *grace*.

Did you expect something more? Don't worry. I'm convinced that you'll come to understand their value as we travel on. But note this well at the beginning of our journey: *The goal of everything is the glory of God, and the means of everything is the grace of God.*

Ponder that for a moment. Don't rush ahead too quickly, for this is the map of the journey.

The *Goal* of Everything Is the *Glory* of God.

Let's take up the first point for a moment and consider it: The goal of everything is the glory of God. How do we know this is true? Because God has said so. He said it early and He said it often. From His first dealings with the Israelites—in the first section of the Bible (Genesis through Deuteronomy, known as the Pentateuch)—God vouchsafed His message with this pledge: "As surely as I live and as surely as the glory of the LORD fills the whole earth . . ." (Num. 14:21).

How certain is what God intends to do? It is as sure as the

living existence of the Lord Himself. It is God's way of saying, "If ever I cease to exist, then you can begin to doubt what I'm telling you now!" That isn't going to happen, for God is eternally self-existing.

What is the stage upon which this absolute certainty will be played out? Simply put, it is "the whole earth." Of all the planets in the farthest reaches of space, this earth has been chosen. Our home—this single orb afloat in a sea of planets, stars and other stellar objects—is center stage! But someone objects, "What about the other planets? How do you know there isn't something else going on out there? How do you know there isn't some other race, some other being, some other world?" Quite simply, because God has said that this planet is center stage for what He is doing in His grand purposes for the universe. I like the way John Piper puts it:

> The space telescope sends back infrared images of faint galaxies perhaps twelve billion light-years away (twelve billion times six trillion miles). Even within our Milky Way, there are stars that are five million times brighter than the sun. The reason for "wasting" so much space on a universe to house a speck of humanity is to make a point about our Maker, not us (Isaiah 19:1). The untracked, unimaginable stretches of the created universe are a parable about the inexhaustible "riches of his glory" (Romans 9:23). The physical eye is meant to say to the spiritual eye, "Not this, but the Maker of this, is the Desire of your soul."
>
> The point is this: We were made to know and treasure the glory of God above all things. The sun of God's glory was made to shine at the center of the solar system of our soul. And when it does, all the planets of our life are held in their proper orbit. But when the sun is displaced, everything flies apart. The healing of the soul begins by restoring the glory of God to its flaming, all-attracting place at the center.
>
> We are all starved for the glory of God, not self. No one goes to the Grand Canyon to increase self-esteem. Why do we

go? Because there is greater healing for the soul in beholding splendor than there is in beholding self. . . . Into the darkness of petty self-preoccupation has shone "the light of *the gospel of the glory of Christ*, who is the image of God" (2 Corinthians 4:4, emphasis added). The Gospel is about "the glory of Christ," not about me (John 17:24). Its final aim is that we would see and savor and show the glory of Christ: "He is the radiance of the glory of God and the exact imprint of his nature" (Hebrews 1:3). When the light of the Gospel shines in our hearts, it is "the light of the knowledge of the glory of God in the face of Christ" (2 Corinthians 4:6).

And when we "rejoice in hope and the glory of God" (Romans 5:2), that hope is "our blessed hope, the appearing of the glory *of our great God* and Savior Jesus Christ" (Titus 2:13, emphasis added).[2]

It is true that earth is center stage for all God's eternal purposes, but on that stage the spotlight falls even more narrowly upon the ones He has placed at the center of center stage—human beings! Human beings are unique among all the creatures God created. We, of all God's creatures, are made in the image of God. We have a unique calling, purpose and destiny. God has said that our meaning is not found in how much we are like others of God's creatures—a line of thought the intellectual community seems obsessed with tracing out. Rather, our meaning is to be found in the other direction—in how much we are like God Himself! So, as Buck Hatch says, the goal of God is to have people filled with the glory of God and living for the glory of God.[3]

This, as I have said, is a theme repeated often throughout the Scriptures. So as we travel down the timeline from the opening books of the Bible, we find the prophets affirming this truth. Habakkuk said, "The earth will be filled with the knowledge of the glory of the LORD, as the waters cover the sea" (2:14). Isaiah similarly declared, "The earth will be full of the knowledge of the LORD as the waters cover the sea" (11:9). The apostle Paul summed up everything from pole to pole by telling the Roman believers, "For from him and through him and to him are all things. To him be the glory forever! Amen" (Rom. 11:36).

Slow down! Did you note this? God is the *source* of all things ("from him"). Everything that exists arises out of God Himself. From His mind, will and actions, all things that make up reality have arisen. God is the *agency* through which all things happen ("through him"). Everything is brought into being and sovereignly controlled by God Himself (Col. 1:16–17). And God is the *destiny* of all things ("to him")—He is the ultimate goal for all that exists. And did you note the conclusion of such all-encompassing thought? "To him be the *glory* forever!"

Truly, the goal of everything is the glory of God.

The *Means* of Everything Is the *Grace* of God

But remember, there are two fixed points necessary to locate our position on this journey from eternity to eternity. The second one reminds us that the gospel is all about the grace of God.

God became a man in the Person of Jesus Christ. Jesus lived perfectly, without sin. When He hung on the cross, the Bible explains that God laid on Him the iniquity of all of us. The guilt for all our sins was placed on Jesus. When He died, He was paying the eternal punishment for who we've been and what we've done. That is grace!

Notice now what the apostle Paul said about this grace: "This grace was given us in Christ Jesus *before the beginning of time*" (2 Tim. 1:9).

What?

You say, "No, I gave my life to Christ and believed in him on such-and-such a date at such-and-such a place." But God says that before anything else existed, He had already thought of you, knew what you'd be and do and had already determined to deal with you in grace by giving His Son as your Savior. That is grace;

that is pure gift. Before you could do one thing good or bad, in the mind and heart of God, Christ had already been sent to the cross on your behalf.

Paul also asserted that "his *eternal* purpose [was] accomplished in Christ Jesus our Lord" (Eph. 3:11). Peter too declared, "[Christ] was chosen *before the creation of the world*, but was revealed in these last times for your sake" (1 Pet. 1:20).

This is true, however, not simply about Jesus as our Savior. It is true of everything in life. Listen to how David prayed: "Everything comes from you, and we have given you only what comes from your hand" (1 Chron. 29:14; see also 1 Cor. 4:7). Paul told the pagan people to whom he preached that God "is not served by human hands, as if he needed anything, because he himself gives all men life and breath and everything else" (Acts 17:25). God gives. He is a God of grace. And this means all things! He is indeed "the God of *all* grace" (1 Pet. 5:10)! Remember, "from him" are all things! (Rom. 11:36).

Jesus is a gift of God's grace. Forgiveness is a gift. Salvation, heaven, eternal life—they are all of grace. But so is the air you're breathing at this moment. And so is that bouncing, red pump thumping in your chest. And so is the wife or husband next to you. And so is . . . well, you fill in the blank. It's *all* a gift. We didn't make any of it—He did! We don't deserve any of it—He does! Yet He created us to share it with Him. That is grace. Such is God. I marvel at the way C.S. Lewis put it: "God who needs nothing, loves into existence wholly superfluous creatures in order that He may love and perfect them."[4]

Every breath you draw in is by means of the grace of God. Every decision you make and every step you take is by God's grace. Every moment you are alive is a gift. Everything you own is a gift. The money in your back pocket or in your purse or lodged in bank accounts or stocks or wherever it is—it's all a gift, on loan from Him. Everything. All of it. Without exception. All of it is by grace.

And there is more: by grace God has a purpose for your life. There is a divinely ordained part that you are to play in His unfolding purposes. Your purpose is found in the relationship of your story to His story. You discover your purpose by discovering how God has designed to uniquely pour grace through your life and, in so doing, move His story along to its final conclusion.

Taking a Reading on Our Position

These, then, are your two fixed points: *glory* and *grace*.

If you travel by these each step along the way, you will conclude at the end of the journey that everything about everything is *about* the *glory* of God. Everything . . . about everything . . . is about the glory of God. That includes how you spend your time, how you make your living, whom you marry, how you raise your kids and how you respond to your parents. It includes how you use your finances, possessions and other resources. It includes what you give your private thoughts to. It includes what or whom you give your love to. What is at issue in the myriad decisions you make each day? Not your pleasure, but God's glory!

You will also conclude that everything about everything is *by* the *grace* of God. Who gave you life? Who gave you time? Who gave you your job? Who gave you the capacity to make wealth? We can keep multiplying the questions, but you get the point. Where did all this come from? From whose hand it is? Why is it distributed to you? How did you come to enjoy these things? These are not yours by right, but by God's grace!

The glory and grace of God are what link your life to the lives of Moses and David and Isaiah and Paul. We, like them, have the privilege of living to enjoy the grace of God and to magnify the glory of God. What is God's purpose for your life? Whatever it is in the specifics, it is about the glory of God. Whatever it is in the minutiae, it is by the grace of God. These are two threads of gold and silver woven into the tapestry of all history. At the end of time, the tapestry will be turned, and we will see that it is those two threads that will connect every part of the story of God—His story, your story.

Where the Story Begins

With that in mind, let's take a look at the place where our journey will soon begin. To do so, I want you to come with me back—far, far back—past the beginning; back into the dark, shrouded, mysterious confines of eternity past. Come back with me past the earthly ministry of Christ, past the days of David, Moses and Abraham, past the days of the Flood and Noah's ark. Press through even the veil of Genesis 1 and 2 and the creation of the universe and the world. Come with me to a time and a place in which the only thing that existed was God.

Technically, it's not even right to speak of it as a time, because time had not yet been created. And, strictly speaking, it's incorrect to call it a place, because neither height, depth, length and breadth nor any spatial dimension had yet been brought into existence. There are no other beings there, no humans, no gods, no angels or demons, no devil. Just God—singular, solitary . . . and utterly satisfied. Here He is—perfect, eternal, unchanging. One God existing from all eternity as Father, Son and Holy Spirit. He is happy and satisfied in that complex of relationships—and always has been. Here is God. Alone. Without deficiency or need.

Strangely, some think God created the world because He was lonely. But He already enjoyed perfect relationships within the fellowship of the Trinity. Others imagine God created the world because He needed something. Was He bored, perhaps? But boredom would imply deficiency and imperfection, and God is and always has been perfect in every way.

So why would a God like this create a world that has become like this? The answer is quite simple, actually. In fact, you already know the answer: glory and grace.

For the sheer pleasure it brought Him to do so, God chose to shine forth the grandeur of His glory by creating a universe full of people and places and peacocks and petunias. He created the landmass upon which your hometown sits. He created the dust that has collected into the as-yet-undetected third moon of some obscure planet in a solar system five hundred billion light-years away. He created all of this. Why? To display His glory and to extend His grace.

God didn't have to. He *wanted* to! He wanted the sheer pleasure of sending out beams of glory from His innermost being. So He spoke, and stars and planets and the earth formed. And He spoke again and . . . well, it all happened! He gave the stars power to shine. He gave the planets orbits to follow. He gave movement to solar systems. He traced the paths electrons chase around the nucleus of their atoms. He gave to the earth living things like orchids and ostriches and orioles.

Did He do all this to fulfill some inner deficiency that had ached long enough? No!

Why then? Because that's the way God is—He is a giving God and a glorious God!

An Infinite Pleasure

But why all this for glory and grace? Hear Isaiah again! "Declaring the end from the beginning, and from ancient times things which have not been done, saying, 'My purpose will be established, and I will accomplish all *My good pleasure*'" (46:10, NASB).

Don't miss the last three words: "My good pleasure." The purpose of everything is related to God's pleasure. My purpose, your purpose is related to God's pleasure. Frankly, this is where we get confused. We are told that it's all about our pleasure. The lie the world tells us is that God is trying to rob us of our pleasure. Not at all! In fact—and again, don't miss this—your highest pleasure is wrapped up in God's greatest pleasure.

How can that be? It is so because God brings glory to Himself by extending grace to you. Your purpose, then, is to employ the grace God extends to you to bring glory to Him. When you figure out how God is investing grace in you and you turn it around to purposefully bring glory to Him, you begin to discover not simply your pleasure but His pleasure.

Think of it! God is infinite; therefore, His pleasure must be boundless as well. God is not seeking to diminish your pleasure, but to infinitely expand it!

If we can rightly say that everything about everything is about the glory of God and that everything about everything is by the grace of God, then we might also accurately say that the atmosphere of everything is the pleasure of God.

The movie *Chariots of Fire* is a dramatized account of the life of Eric Liddell, Scotland's great Olympic champion. Liddell was born in China to missionary parents, then went home to England during his years of schooling. He became convinced of God's call upon his life to return to China for a lifetime of service to God. In fact, he did eventually return and there died at a young age from a cancerous brain tumor. But God had not only created Eric to be a missionary; He had also given him amazing athletic abilities. There is a moving scene in the film in which Eric's sister Jenny is fretting over all the time and attention he is giving to running. She is worried that he will lose sight of God's call upon his life to China. Eric answers her with the immortal words, "God made me for China. But God also made me fast, and when I run, I feel *His pleasure.*"

God has, by His grace, invested certain gifts in you to be used for His glory. You have been given a divinely designed part in God's story. When you begin to identify how God has invested and is investing His grace uniquely in you and you start to use that grace for the eternal purposes of God's glory, you too will be able to say, "When I do _____ (whatever it is for you), I feel His pleasure!"

Again, please understand, God is not against your pleasure.

God is not seeking to minimize your enjoyment of life. He is seeking rather to save you from puny, passing, ultimately disappointing gratifications. He wants to rescue you from being far too easily satisfied with momentary, fleeting things. He wants you to enter into *His pleasure*—a pleasure that is not gone as quickly as the food is swallowed or the sex is over or the spotlight moves from you to someone else. He wants to draw you into the unceasing flow of His eternal joy.

God has a place in His plan for you. That place involves a purpose bigger than you've ever imagined. It involves a gain bigger than you've ever dreamed. It involves a pleasure more intense than you've ever fantasized.

Writing Your Story

Before we move ahead, let's pause and consider how all this helps us understand and write our own personal stories. We need to recognize that you and I can miss all this infinite pleasure of God in any number of ways. First, we can miss God's purpose by doing the *wrong thing*—like being a pastor rather than a plumber, or vice versa. We can also miss God's purpose by doing the *right thing* for the *wrong reason*—our own glory rather than His. And thirdly, we can miss God's purpose by doing the *right thing* with the *wrong resources*—our strength rather than His grace.

Here's the point of this introductory study: *When you do the right thing* (God's will for your life) *for the right reason* (God's glory) *and with the right resources* (God's grace), *you find not just your pleasure, but you enter into His pleasure!*

We've taken but one baby step on this journey from eternity past into eternity future. We haven't even reached Genesis 1 yet, but we will soon enough. For now, keep these two constants before you: God's glory and God's grace. I promise you, everything about everything you face as you close the book on this chapter will be about the glory of God. And everything about everything

He requires of you as you step forward will be by the grace of God. As you keep these fixed constants in view, your life will contribute to and move with God's great, eternal story, even at moments when you feel perhaps that you've lost your way.

Reviewing God's Story

Take a few minutes now to review God's story as we understand it to this point. Nailing down these basics will make for a smoother journey with even greater discoveries as we move forward.

1. What are the two fixed points that will always enable you to find your place, no matter where you are in God's story?

    _____

    _____

2. Complete these two axioms:

    The goal of everything is the _____ of God.

    The means of everything is the _____ of God.

3. Though there is much we don't yet know about God's story, this much we do know: Everything about everything is _____ the glory of God, and everything about everything is _____ the grace of God.

4. I can miss God's purpose for my life by . . .

    Doing the _____ thing.

    Doing the right thing for the wrong _____.

    Doing the right thing with the wrong _____.

5. When I do the right _____ (God's will for
    my life) for the right _____ (God's glory)
    and with the right _____ (God's grace),
    I find not just my pleasure, but I enter into God's
    _____!

Remembering God's Story

Scriptures	Eternity past (pre-Genesis 1)

Key Character	God and God alone

Key Events	The eternal decrees of God

Key Verses	"Remember the former things, those of long ago; I am God and there is no other; I am God, and there is none like me. I make known the end from the beginning, from ancient times, what is still to come. I say: My purpose will stand, and I will do all that I please." Isaiah 46:9–10

Eternity Past

Eternity Future

God's Story

PART 2

HIS STORY

God made man because He loves stories.
—**Elie Wiesel**

History is a story written by the finger of God.
—**C.S. Lewis**

All history is incomprehensible without Christ.
—**Joseph Ernest Renan**

The Scripture stories do not, like Homer's, court our favor; they do not flatter us that they may please us and enchant us; they seek to subject us, and if we refuse to be subjected, we are rebels.
—**Erich Auerbach**

The Stage Set

A Spurned Grace
Genesis 1–11

My son Clint had an encounter with a philosopher a while back. At the time, Clint was in the fourth grade; the philosopher was two grades behind. The encounter took place on the school bus as it headed for home. He overheard this deep-thinking little girl as she queried the bus driver: "Who made God?"

We may chuckle inwardly, but this little girl, with only seven years of experience in life, was asking a deep question—one that would frame her perception of reality for the rest of her life. She was asking a worldview question. She wouldn't have known to call it that, but she was asking about a fundamental issue that would soon gel into the assumptions, presuppositions and unexamined "givens" about how she views reality.

You too have a worldview. Like it or not. Know it or not. We all do. Your worldview is the grid of ideas, beliefs and presumptions through which you read the world and relate within it. Or, more simply stated, a worldview is the set of lenses through which you perceive the world. The question is not whether you have a worldview—rather, it is whether or not your worldview is accurate. Is it in line with reality? Are you looking at the world through the right set of lenses? Do you perceive reality, or is your soul's sight distorted and skewed?

Many North Americans have tried to "accept Christ" as their Savior and, at the same time, to retain their non-Christian worldview. This creates great conflict within. It is a bit like how we enjoy Chinese food. We Americans love to go out for Chinese, but most of us have never been to China and have no intention of going there, let alone adopting a Chinese worldview.

Christ and the salvation He offers are not selections from a menu which you can piece together according to your whims and tastes and personal desires. Christ's salvation means utter abandonment to the God of all things, the Lord of time—the Creator, Sustainer and Director of all that is. As the saying goes, if Christ is not Lord of all, He is not Lord at all. Thus the conflict: the worldview most of us have inherited does not afford Christ that exalted place. Is it possible you have afforded Him an important place, maybe even a very significant position, but have not made Him the Lord of everything?

What then does the Bible disclose about the purpose, direction and culmination of history? Is history really His story? Is God sovereignly in control, weaving all of reality into a tapestry that will in the end reveal a coherent plan that has been pursued each step along the way? Or is this a world of random chaotic nonsense, headed nowhere, meaning nothing? And what does my choice of worldview do to my personal sense of purpose and place in this world and in God's plan?

Step Back to Step Forward

This drama will take us from eternity past to eternity future. So let's go back to the beginning—to the opening books of Scripture—where we've already started to position ourselves. But as we take our place, make sure you recall the tip I gave you for this journey. Remembering your two determined points will help you find your way and orient yourself to reality along this journey from eternity to eternity. As with a mariner's sextant, aligning yourself with these two fixed constants will help you orient yourself to reality and to what is taking place around you.

Fix your thoughts for a moment on the two treasures, glory and grace. And once more, settle these truths firmly in your mind: No matter where you are in history or what you are observing, everything about everything is *about* the glory of God, and everything about everything is *by* the grace of God.

So, come with me far, far back to the beginning of it all—actually past the beginning. Go with me into the dark, shrouded, mysterious confines of eternity past—to a time when there was no time, to a place where there was as yet no place—where the only thing that existed was God.

There He is! Singular, solitary, utterly satisfied in Himself. Perfect, eternal and unchanging. The one and only God, existing from all eternity as Father, Son and Holy Spirit—happy and satisfied in that complex of relationships. Here is God, alone, without deficiency or need.

Now, having arrived mentally in eternity past, take your Bible in hand and open to the first page of Scripture—Genesis 1. But do you realize that we have already positioned ourselves even further back than "the beginning" that Genesis 1:1 describes? Having slipped behind the curtain of time and space, we are in a place described in John 1:1—which takes us further back than Genesis 1:1! Genesis 1:1 says, "In the beginning God created the heavens and the earth." But John 1:1 says, "In the beginning was the Word, and the Word was with God, and the Word was God."

Here He is—One God, eternally in three Persons. Not bored, not deficient or imperfect, but enjoying perfect relationship within the fellowship of the Trinity.

What Was God Thinking?

So again, if God has everything He needs and is totally satisfied in Himself, why would He create a world that has become the way it is? Look one more time at those constants: glory and grace! God created because His basic nature is glorious and gracious. For the sheer pleasure it brought Him, He spoke the word and created (for His glory), and He speaks and sustains (by His grace) all things by that word.

But why glory and grace? Why are these so important? Because God glorifies Himself most when He is being gracious to the world He created—and that includes, by the way, you! It brings God pleasure to extend His grace.

But we are getting ahead of ourselves. Let me be the first to welcome you to eternity past! Look around. You'll note that there is no up or down, black or white, backward or forward. There is no earth, no sun, no light or darkness. There are no angels or demons, and no devil. No air, no water and no fire. No humans and no rabbits, cattle or walruses. The only thing that exists is God. He has been forever.

So our little philosopher's question was wrongly framed from the beginning. No one made God—He possesses eternal self-existence within Himself! As such, He does not need time, for He is eternally timeless. He does not require space and place, for He is spirit. He does not need people, for He enjoys the perfect, happy, eternally fulfilling relationships within His own divine being—Father, Son and Holy Spirit. He is the uncaused Causer of all that is!

I know this may be a bit overwhelming. Take a deep breath. Steady yourself. Now, consider this: somewhere back here something happened—a decision was made. Since there is nothing here except God, that something had to have happened within God, and it had to have happened by His own choice. In what is for us the mysterious, fog-shrouded reality of eternity past, God activated His will. That will—God's will—set reality into being.

As the Bible opens, Genesis 1–11 frames for us the basic nature of reality. Before the curtain rises and the opening act of God's unfolding drama begins to play out before our eyes, God first sets the stage. He does so through these first eleven chapters.

The nature of reality in the earth as we know it—the reality in which we now live—is framed for us through four key words.

Creation

The first word is *creation*. God describes the creation of the heavens and the earth and all they contain in the first two chapters of Genesis. Through God's creation of the universe, we find His glory displayed and His grace extended.

There is, as you know, a great deal of debate about the matter of origins. Before you let your mind wander too far down that trail of debate, stop and look at Genesis 1–2. As you stare down at the pages of your Bible that comprise these two chapters, think for a moment about what they contain. Think about Genesis 1 and 2 *proportionately*. Ask yourself, Why does the first book of the Bible contain only two chapters describing the creation of the cosmos and yet give thirty-nine chapters to the story of one man and his family?[1] (See Genesis 11–50.) Do you realize that God later devotes two entire chapters of His Holy Scriptures to dealing with infectious skin diseases, mildew and rot (Lev. 13–14)—as much space as He here gives to describing the creation of all that is?

The proportionality of Genesis 1 and 2 tells us something significant. God's account of the origin of the universe is correct, historically reliable and accurate—but it is selective. Indeed, the whole of the Bible is selective. Everything God has told us in Scripture is true, reliable and sufficient. Yet God has not told us everything there is to be said about reality. How could an infinite God make His mind entirely known to finite creatures? God is reliable in His revelation, but He is also selective.

So we must ask, why has God told us the things He *has* spoken to us? He is speaking a particular message to us. He is saying something to us in Genesis 1–2. What is God telling us here?

For one thing, God is telling us that reality is not the product of natural forces, but of the will of the sovereign God. The

Bible, you will note, does not even attempt to argue the existence of God. It does not set forth an apologetic argument for His being and presence in the universe. The Bible simply begins with a Person: "In the beginning God . . ."

If those opening four words of Scripture are true, then it tells us that *atheism* is in error, for God is and predates everything else that is. It also tells us that *pantheism*—the idea that God is indistinguishable from the physical world—is in error, for He predates, is separate from and is the origin of all that is. Additionally, *polytheism* is wrong. There are not many gods—there is from the beginning only one sovereign God. If the words "In the beginning God . . ." are true, then it means that *materialism* is false, for before the material world existed, there was the eternal, timeless God. It also means that *dualism* is wrong. Dualism is the notion that there are two equal and opposite forces at work in the world—good and evil. In this mode of thinking, all of creation is wringing its hands, wondering which force will win in the end. No, the Bible says that from the start there was only one God—holy, just, benevolent and good. Equally, *humanism* must be in error, for before man was God, and from God man arose. And if the Bible's opening line is correct, then *naturalism* is in error, for God's will is the origin of all that exists.[2]

Again, stop—take a deep breath. Look about you. You'll find nothing but God. And you'll find that He is eternal (before anything else was, God was), self-existent (nothing caused God; He is the uncaused Causer of all things), sovereign (everything arose out of God, nothing exists except by His will, and all things continue and are preserved by His own continuous, powerful word) and personal (*Elohim*, a plural noun, while not proving the Trinity, points us in the direction of the later revelation of the Scriptures which do teach the triune nature of God).

"In the beginning God . . ." In short, the whole of creation is about God's glory! "The heavens declare the glory of God; the skies proclaim the work of his hands" (Ps. 19:1). "Since the creation of the world God's invisible qualities—his eternal power and divine nature—have been clearly seen, being understood from what has been made" (Rom. 1:20).

But there is something more that we learn about this magnificent Person—His word is unspeakably powerful. The world all about us was *spoken* into being! Repeatedly throughout the opening chapter of Scripture, we discover that "God said" (1:3, 6, 9, 11, 14, 20, 24, 26, 29). And every time God opened His mouth to speak, something new burst into existence!

We are told that the universe contains something like one hundred billion galaxies. It has been estimated that the total mass of the universe is in the vicinity of a trillion, trillion, trillion, trillion tons of matter! Think about it. One second there was nothing. Not one ounce. Not one gram. One second later (if I can borrow a word from the created world of time and space), after a word from God, all the mass and energy of the universe existed!

What kind of a *word* can do such a thing?

Scripture unashamedly declares that "the worlds were prepared by the word of God" (Heb. 11:3, NASB). The psalmist said, "By the word of the LORD were the heavens made, their starry host by the breath of his mouth. . . . For he spoke, and it came to be; he commanded, and it stood firm" (33:6, 9). Remember, "In the beginning was the Word, and the Word was with God, and the Word was God. He was with God in the beginning. Through him all things were made; without him nothing was made that has been made" (John 1:1–3).

How awesome must this word be?

One thing we know with certainty about this universe in which we find ourselves: there is a Voice speaking. Further, we can expect that this Voice is telling us of God's purpose. "The facts are," said A.W. Tozer, "that God is not silent, has never been silent. It is the nature of God to speak. The second Person of the Holy Trinity is called the Word. The Bible is the inevitable outcome of God's continuous speech. It is the infallible declaration of His mind for us put into our familiar human words."[3]

And it is this Word which "became flesh and made his dwelling among us. We have seen his [Are you ready for this? Remember those fixed points!] *glory*, the *glory* of the One and Only, who came from the Father, full of [you guessed it!] *grace* and truth" (John 1:14).

So far this Word has told us that before anything else was, God was—gracious and glorious. Our entire universe arose out of His will and by His voice. This creation arose by His grace and is primarily designed as a stage for the demonstration of His glory.

But chapters one and two of Genesis tell us not only about the reality of the universe and of God, but about the reality of our own makeup and humanity. What does this Word tell us about ourselves?

We were created to be something uniquely special among all God's creatures. We are made in the image of God (Gen. 1:26–27). We possess by God's design a unique relational dimension—for the triune God made us in His image. We have a unique moral dimension—for the holy God made us in His image. We have been created with a unique personal dimension—for the God who Himself possesses mind, emotions and will fashioned us according to His image. We have a unique creational dimension—for the creator God formed us in His image. We cannot, like God, create from nothing, but we can take what He has created and display—to His glory—a remarkable and helpful creativity. And we possess a unique spiritual dimension—for God who is Spirit has made us in His image.

We were also created to do something uniquely special in God's world. We are called to reproduce and to rule (1:28). We are to reproduce, filling the world with people committed to the glory of God and living by the grace of God. We are to work under God's authority to bring His dominion to every part of His created world—magnifying His glory and extending His grace.

For all of this to take place, God fashioned a perfect world and placed us in it (2:4–17). God's verdict over all that He made was repeatedly, "Good!" (1:4, 10, 12, 18, 21, 25). Indeed, when He rested from His creative work, He declared it "very good" (1:31)!

Yes, it was "very good" . . . but not for long. For, sadly, the record of Scripture introduces the second word that frames our understanding of reality.

Coup

Genesis 3:1–13 describes for us a deliberate, organized coup arising from among the creatures God had made. They tried to throw off the sovereign rule of their Creator. In so doing, the created defied the Creator's glory and rejected His grace. The grim figure behind this coup is the tempter: "Now the serpent was more crafty than any of the wild animals the LORD God had made" (3:1).

Wait a minute! When did he enter the picture? you may ask. I don't recall anything about him in the first two chapters.

You are right about that. The fact is, the Bible doesn't tell us exactly when the tempter—the devil or Satan—was created. But we do know that he was created by God and given a primary place in God's glorious presence (Ezek. 28:14). At some point he lusted after God's glory and desired to take it as his own (Isa. 14:13–15), and because of that God banished him from His presence. Ever since that time, the devil has been seeking to rob God of His glory and to deprive God's people of His grace.

Taking just what we know thus far about the fabric of reality, how do you suppose such a tempter seeks to go about his work? His first, and still principal, tactic is to introduce *questions about God's Word*: "Did God really say, 'You must not eat from any tree in the garden'?" (Gen. 3:1). Imagine! He tries to trump the Word that created and rules the universe! He seeks to undermine the very Word by which he was created and which now sustains his continuing existence (along with that of all created reality; see Heb. 1:3)!

He also incites us to *add to God's Word*. Notice the subtle shift as Eve refers to God's command: "God did say, 'You must not eat fruit from the tree that is in the middle of the garden, and *you must not touch it*, or you will die.'" (Gen. 3:3). God's instructions made no mention of touching the tree.

Then also the Evil One woos us to *weaken God's Word*. God's "you will *surely* die" (2:17) became a mere "you will die" (3:3) on the tempted woman's tongue.

The woman gave the inward consent of her will (3:6) and quickly began to reap the inward consequences of her willfulness (3:7). Instantly she could *see* something she had not noticed before. See what? That pleasure might be enjoyed just for itself, not as a shared experience with God: "The woman saw the fruit of the tree was . . . pleasing to the eye" (3:6). Not only could she and the man now see, but just as quickly both of them were seen. Seen as what? As they had become in their selfishness: "Then the eyes of both of them were opened, and they realized they were naked" (3:7). Quickly their *shame* became self-apparent: "So they sewed fig leaves together and made coverings for themselves" (3:7).

Besides the tempter, there is another figure standing over the entire scene—the Tester. After Adam and Eve sinned against Him, God asked four questions to expose the seismic catastrophe that had shaken the universe. He is still putting these questions to the hearts of rebels everywhere. God asked and still asks questions inviting *relationship*: "Where are you?" (3:9). He asked and still asks questions inviting *honesty*: "Who told you"? (3:11). He asked and still asks questions inviting *responsibility*: "Have you eaten"? (3:11). He asked and asks still questions inviting *confession*: "What is this you have done?" (3:13).

The encounter in the Garden is historical and factual: it actually happened. It is also prototypical: it happens still. The Evil One perpetuates the same lies and temptations, and we perpetuate the same disastrous choices. All this leads us to ask, With a Creator like this, in a world as He created it, what will become of the creatures' coup? Will there be consequences?

Can there fail to be consequences? Can God's glory be soiled and His grace spurned with impunity?

Consequences

God's glory had been defied and His grace rejected. As the inevitable consequences begin to manifest themselves, we will now find God's glory demonstrated and His grace protected (3:14–11:9). If you stand back from these chapters in Genesis and observe carefully, you just might make out the ripples on the pond of humanity as they spread to the furthest shores of human experience. Here we will observe individual humans at odds with God personally, and then mankind as a whole at odds with Him collectively.

Take note of the *personal alienation* that came from Adam and Eve's rebellion (3:15–24): The serpent is alienated from the other creatures (3:14–15). Then the woman is alienated from the man (3:16), the man from his work (3:17–19), and the man and woman from God (3:23–24). They are banished from Eden, and the way back to God's glorious presence is closed and guarded.

Personal alienation bred *personal violence* (4:1–26): Cain killed Abel (4:1–12). Strange, is it not, that the first murder was religiously motivated? Violence then bred more violence—for Cain was convinced that his murder would return upon his own head (4:13–16). In fact, just three generations later Lamech killed two men and promised that more murders would follow if anyone tried to hold him accountable (4:23–24).

The violence spread until human society was characterized by *collective wickedness* (Gen. 6–9):

The LORD saw how great man's wickedness on the earth had
become, and that every inclination of the thoughts of his
heart was only evil all the time. The LORD was grieved that
he had made man on the earth, and his heart was filled with
pain. . . . Now the earth was corrupt in God's sight and was
full of violence. God saw how corrupt the earth had become,
for all the people on earth had corrupted their ways. So God
said to Noah, "I am going to put an end to all people, for the
earth is filled with violence because of them. I am surely going
to destroy both them and the earth." (6:5–6, 11–13)

God, grieving over His spurned grace and jealous over His
soiled glory, determined to wipe the globe clean and to begin
again—with just eight people. God's choice was based on His
grace: "Noah found grace in the eyes of the LORD" (6:8, NKJV).
And as His grace always does, it resulted in righteousness: "Noah
was a righteous man, blameless among the people of his time,
and he walked with God" (6:9). But by the end of his story, even
Noah had spurned God's grace and rejected God's righteousness:
"Noah, a man of the soil, proceeded to plant a vineyard. When
he drank some of its wine, he became drunk and lay uncovered
inside his tent" (9:20–21). So the account of God's redo ends
with another curse being pronounced (9:22–25).

The collective wickedness then culminates in the dream of
a *secular utopia* (11:1–9). "Then they said, 'Come, let us build
ourselves a city, with a tower that reaches to the heavens, so that
we may make a name for ourselves and not be scattered over the
face of the whole earth.'" (11:4). These descendants of Noah
rejected a God-dependent grace and embraced self-reliance: "Let
us build ourselves a city." They again rejected God's glory and
sought a glory of their own: ". . . that we may make a name for
ourselves." They stiff-armed God's commandment to "be fruitful
and increase in number and fill the earth" (9:1), and demanded
they would "not be scattered over the face of the whole earth."
But God intervened in their plans:

So the LORD scattered them from there over all the earth,
and they stopped building the city. That is why it was called
Babel—because there the LORD confused the language of the
whole world. From there the LORD scattered them over the
face of the whole earth. (11:8–9)

Interestingly, the name Babel means the "gate of the gods."
These headstrong people believed they could have God on their
own terms. The word "confused" (Hebrew, *bālal*) sounds a bit
like Babel—the message is that their greatest rallying point became a scene of utter chaos! And it will always be so wherever we
seek to establish our own man-centered, God-rejected utopia.

These same consequences continue to ripple further and further out to the far banks of our own lives and of the societies we
have created. In the words of Rodney King, which he uttered
in the wake of the bloody riots that racked Los Angeles after
his ruthless beating at the hands of police, "Can't we all just get
along?" The answer, if we have any sense of history, is "Obvi-
ously not!" Hopeful social contractors feeling their way along
with their white canes demand, "We can figure this thing out!"
But God will not allow it.

OK. Take a few deep breaths!

Now, be honest. The picture at this point is pretty grim. But
I urge you to remember that the stage is only being set for God's
first great act in this unfolding drama. And even in this prelude
to our journey, this forbidding tone is not the last note sounded.

Covenant

If you are a careful reader, you may have noticed that thus far
in our overview of Genesis 1–11, we have not touched on some
of the things mentioned in the passage. But the wind of the
Spirit blows through the sections of Scripture we have missed,
sounding in each of them a note of hope. It is precisely in those
places that God's glory is defended and His grace extended once
again (3:15; 5; 10; 11:10–32).

The first ringing of hope sounds forth in the immediate aftermath of sin. God announces to the serpent, "I will put enmity between you and the woman, and between your offspring [lit., "seed"] and hers; he will crush your head, and you will strike his heel" (3:15). This is called the *protoevangelium*, or the first gospel. Indeed, the good news proclaimed here was fulfilled in Christ (Heb. 2:14–15; 1 John 3:8)! With this promise from God, Adam and Eve eagerly watched for the coming "seed." They likely believed the arrival of their first son, Cain, had brought the birth of their redeemer. Imagine their double grief when the one they had staked their hopes upon proved to be a murderer!

The note of hope, however, is sounded again and again in the spaces of Genesis 1–11. We find in these chapters three genealogies (Gen. 5, 10, 11:10–32), which actually have something to say to us. The casual reader who picks up a Bible and starts reading at the beginning may ask, why are these here? But the careful reader recognizes them as notes of hope, for they trace the line of the original promise of a redeemer.

Take note of the first genealogy in Genesis 5: "This is the written account of Adam's line. When God created man, he made him in the likeness of God. He created them male and female and blessed them. And when they were created, he called them 'man'" (5:1–2). Why summarize the creation account here five chapters into the book? Because the writer is signaling that he is picking up the story after an interruption, and his purpose in adding this list of names is to help us connect the dots to God's plan and purpose.

Who do we find in this list of names? Note the first one: "When Adam had lived 130 years, he had a son in his own likeness, in his own image; and he named him Seth" (5:3). The name Seth means "granted"—or we might say *grace*! Even with the devastation and chaos of sin, God has a plan to continue extending His grace! The redeemer to come will be "granted" through the line of Seth.

The genealogy of Genesis 5 ends with Noah (5:29–32). What have we already learned about God's dealings with this man? "Noah found grace in the eyes of the LORD" (6:8, NKJV). The narrative then details the story of Noah in chapters 6 through 9. That brings us to the next hopeful note.

The second genealogy, in Genesis 10, details the new start of the family tree of humanity. Noah is the trunk (10:1), and his three sons are the branches: Japheth (10:2–5), Ham (10:6–20) and Shem (10:21–31). We have already been alerted to a promise of grace (3:16), and we've been signaled that it will be fulfilled through the line of Seth (5:3). True to form, several generations later we find that "Noah found grace in the eyes of the LORD."

So?

Look at how the third genealogy begins: "This is the account of Shem" (11:10). Connect the dots: the promise to Adam and Eve (3:15) . . . Seth ("granted") . . . Noah ("found grace in the eyes of the LORD") . . . Noah's son Shem. As the final pieces are placed upon the stage in preparation for the opening curtain on Act I, Scene 1 of God's drama of redemption, God now drops the house lights and centers a single spotlight, narrowing its focus upon one man, who will come from the line of Shem. The lingering promise that begs to be fulfilled through him brings the onlookers to the ready. So who will we find in this long list of names who closes in the frame of reality?

The names proceed one after the other, as we have come to expect in these genealogies, until they come to the last name: Abram (10:27). That name may not mean much if you don't know at least something about the drama that will follow. But let me tip you off to a bit of the suspense of Act I, Scene 1: *Abram will be chosen as the line through which grace will be extended and glory demonstrated to all of creation!*

Now the stage is set for Act I in God's unfolding drama. He has gone from dealing with all of humanity, narrowing it down to just one man through whom He will pour out His grace—in order that His grace might come once again to all people. This is the first major step in time and space toward the fulfillment of the purpose of God, which He put in motion in eternity past. God has the goal clearly in sight: "Truly, as I live, all the earth shall be filled with the glory of the LORD" (Num. 14:21, NKJV).

Writing Your Story

What's that? Do I hear someone raising an objection?

That has a lot to do with God's story, but I'm not hearing much about my story! you might say. *What about your promise of finding my place in God's plan?*

OK, fair enough. I'll let you in on a secret. Are you ready?

The opening of Act II (the New Testament era) begins in precisely the same way that Act I opens—with a genealogy! "A record of the genealogy [literally, "genesis"] of Jesus Christ the Son of David, the son of *Abraham*" (Matt. 1:1). God is inviting us to connect the dots and observe the pattern of His unfolding plan!

God is drawing a line from Genesis 11 to Matthew 1:1. It is not that the Old Testament history between these two points is unimportant. God simply wants to make certain that you see the line of purpose He pursues in all that transpires from Abraham to Christ.

Suffice it to say, as the curtain opens on Act I, we see that God has set the stage for *something* that He will still be doing in the time of Christ. It is the same *something* God is still doing today, and it is that *something* which is the key to your personal story. Maybe I shouldn't jump ahead, but here's a small hint from the New Testament: "If you [that means *you*!] belong to Christ, then you [put your name here] are Abraham's seed, and heirs according to the promise" (Gal. 3:29).

Can you see it? The faint image of your story is already starting to emerge.

So in view of these things, consider this question: *Do I belong to Christ?* I can assure you that this is the most fundamental question that all of us must answer.

Before you close the book on this chapter, breathe a prayer with me: "Oh Lord, please, by your Spirit, help me connect the dots so I can see Your plan and my place in it! Amen!"

Reviewing God's Story

1. Name the four words which frame reality:

    C_____

    C_____

    C_____

    C_____

2. If the first four words of the Bible are true, what "isms" are denounced as erroneous?

    A_____

    P_____

    P_____

    M_____

    D_____

    H_____

    N_____

3. What is the three-fold strategy of the tempter with regard to God's Word?

    Q_____ God's Word

    A_____ to God's Word

W_____ God's Word

4. What are the four primary questions God is still putting to
   us today?

   "Where are you?"_____

   "Who told you . . . ?"_____

   "Have you eaten . . . ?"_____

   "What is this you have done?"_____

5. Describe the descending steps of chaos as humanity tries to
   deal with the consequences of rebellion against God.

   Personal _____

   Personal _____

   Collective _____

   Secular _____

Remembering God's Story

Scriptures	Genesis 1–11

Key Characters	God, Adam and Eve, the serpent, Cain and Abel, Seth, Noah, Shem

Key Events	Creation, Fall, expulsion from Eden, murder of Abel, Flood, Babel

Key Verses	"In the beginning was the Word, and the Word was with God, and the Word was God. . . . Through him all things were made. . . . The Word became flesh and made his dwelling among us. We have seen his glory, the glory of the One and Only, full of grace and truth." John 1:1, 3, 14

Eternity Past

Creation

Fall into sin

Flood

Tower of Babel

Gen. 1–11

God's Story

Eternity Future

ACT 1, SCENE 1

A Pursuing Grace
Genesis 12–1 Kings 10

The stage has been set. The house lights flicker, signaling the audience to find their places and take their seats. As they do, conversations grow hushed and the lights are brought low, except for a single spotlight fixed upon the stage. A rush of excitement rises in each heart, fanned by the curiosity of what will be seen when the curtain is lifted.

Up to this point, we have been situating ourselves in a place where we can look in a panoramic way at the drama of God's redemptive story. We have been seeking to observe the broad sweep of the story God is writing across human history. And, of course, we hope to find how each of our individual stories fit in the midst of His.

The stage has been prepared for Act I in this drama. Crack open your Bible to Genesis 12, and watch now as the curtain of God's readied stage begins to rise.

As the curtain flutters, remember the goal God has established: "Truly, as I live, all the earth shall be filled with the glory of the Lord" (Num. 14:21, NKJV). And remember the two absolutes He has given for our journey: glory and grace. They will always be true, fixed, constant, sure guides in our journey from eternity past to eternity future!

Genesis 1–11 set the stage by presenting God's gracious and

glorious creation of a perfect universe and world, which were then spoiled by rebellion and a grasping after glory. Man chose to live on his own resources rather than God's grace. We looked on as the ripple effects of that rebellion began to move out across the entire surface of humanity.

What is God's plan to reverse the curse and, in so doing, to display His glory and extend His grace? That's the question left lingering in our minds. Now, as the curtain opens, the gracious and glorious answer is about to be played out before our eyes. So let me now, even as the drama begins to unfold, state that plan in one succinct sentence so we will better understand the progress of God's work as it plays out. Are you ready? Here it is: *God's plan is to use one man (Abraham) to build one great nation (Israel) through whom He will provide the one Savior (Jesus) who will reveal God's glory and extend God's grace to ALL people!*

That is God's redemptive plan. So take your Bible in hand and behold Act I, Scene 1 of God's unfolding drama of redemption. We will find in it a pursuing grace. Act I, Scene 1 is described in Genesis 12 through First Kings 10. Put your finger in Genesis 12 and your thumb at First Kings 10. Notice how large a section of Scripture and history you will be traveling through in the next few minutes.

I'm going to warn you now—it will be easy to become lost and confused in reading such a vast section of Scripture. So remember that God is moving with a single purpose through all those pages, across all those chapters and in every one of those verses. God is starting with one man and building one great nation.

We can track His progress toward this goal by finding eight God-sized strides across the landscape of these pages, years, people and places. At each divine footprint we'll stop and observe in it a lasting principle that will help us as we each seek to find our own story in the context of God's story.

Step #1: A Man (Genesis 12:1–3)

The first step is God's selection of a man. To save the entire world, God began with just one man.

Remember how throughout Genesis 4–11 God kept narrowing the field from dealing with all of mankind as a whole to finally choosing just one person? God never stopped loving all people. He never, even for a moment, ceased to desire the redemption of all mankind. But God chose this one man so as to bring grace to all people. Thus, we read:

> The LORD had said to Abram, "Leave your country, your people and your father's household and go to the land I will show you. I will make you into a great nation and I will bless you; I will make your name great, and you will be a blessing. I will bless those who bless you, and whoever curses you I will curse; and all peoples on earth will be blessed through you." (12:1–3)

God called Abram by His *glory*: "The God of glory appeared to our father Abraham while he was still in Mesopotamia, before he lived in Haran" (Acts 7:2). And God called Abram by His *grace*. We know so because in these first three verses of Genesis 12, we find some form of the word "bless" five times! And six times God says, "I will"! This is God's doing, and it is all by grace.

But why Abram? Some people believe there must have been something special about him. They reason that there must have been something within Abram that moved God to choose him. They may believe he possessed a superior spiritual nature or had already proven himself as a seeker of God. All such assumptions miss the point. The fact is that Abram had been an idolatrous pagan like everyone else around him. There was one basis (and only one) upon which God chose this man: grace!

Now consider the promises God made to Abram. God promised to make him "into a great nation" (12:2) and to give him his own land, telling him, "Go to the land I will show you" (12:1).

God will repeat, reaffirm and expand this covenant in Genesis 15 and 17. Here's some counsel: throughout the Old Testament watch these two themes—*nation* and *land*. And don't ever get lost regarding where they fit in the great scheme of what God is doing—to use one man (Abraham) to build one great nation (Israel) through whom He will provide the one Savior (Jesus) who will reveal God's glory and extend God's grace to all people!

As we gaze upon this impressive footprint in the sands of history, take note of our first principle: *When God wants to do a great thing, He graces one person that He might grace many more people.*

None of us are Abram. He, by God's grace, holds a unique place in God's plan. But there is something prototypical about how God dealt with Abram. God follows much of the same pattern with all His people: grace to one—not because the one is superior or special—but in order to make that one a channel of grace to many others. It is always about God's glory and grace. While it is true that God loves you, His work is never just about you. Don't ever forget it!

Step #2: A Family (Genesis 12–50)

Now, if one man is going to become a great nation, where would God likely start? You'd figure the man needs a wife. And indeed, he has one.

But these two have no children! If you were starting with one man in order to build a great nation, you'd need a baby so that at least you'd have a family to start working with. So step number two is the story of God taking this barren, elderly couple and supernaturally giving them a child of promise. This is the story of God growing this one couple into a family.

After chapter 11, the rest of Genesis is about the building of Abraham's family. Genesis 12–24 contains the story of Abram (soon to become Abraham). His son Isaac's story is found in Genesis 25–27; his grandson Jacob's story is found in Genesis

27–50; and his great-grandson Joseph's story completes the book in Genesis 37–50.

Remember I told you to keep in mind the proportionality of Genesis. Just two chapters on creation; thirty-nine chapters on one family! Why? Because God is not as interested in sharing the details of how He created the world as in revealing how He is working to redeem and restore that world.

In breaking down the story of Abraham's family, we find the promises (covenant) God had made to Abraham repeated, reaffirmed and expanded to his son Isaac (26:3–4) and later to his grandson Jacob (28:13–15). It makes sense that God would record this. But why the story of Joseph?

Joseph is not the son of Abraham, but of Jacob. So why is his story so prominent? It's because he is an important link in the purposes of God. Joseph's story (Gen. 37–50) tells how God kept that promise He had made to Abraham and that He had repeated and expanded to Isaac and Jacob! Through Joseph we learn that God never forgets a promise—even through our darkest hours! After years of seeming confusion and abandonment, Joseph could say to his brothers who had abused and misused him, "You intended to harm me, but God intended it for good to accomplish what is now being done, the saving of many lives" (50:20). What faith! Despite long gaps in the divine storyline, Joseph began to see God's enduring purpose shine through!

Here, then, is our second principle: *God never loses track of His promises, and He works even in our darkest hours to redeem them and to fulfill His good purpose through us.* I'm guessing this may be a principle you need to apply already. As you look at the pattern of your life, you may see no discernable scheme or purpose, certainly nothing you'd be willing to label as divine. Yet even in the darkness, God never loses sight of His promises to you.

So, we've come to the end of Genesis. How is the progress in God's purpose coming along? Do we have a great nation? No.

What do we have? We have a family of seventy people (46:26–27). Not a nation—a family! But it's a start.

Now from the orchestra pit the cello sounds an ominous note. This little family is facing difficult days—four hundred years' worth of days (15:13–16)! Will they survive? Will God's purpose prevail?

Step #3: A People (Exodus 1)

As we turn the page to Exodus 1, what do we find? The family, because of hardship, has had to leave their land and go into Egypt:

> These are the names of the sons of Israel who went to Egypt with Jacob, each with his family: Reuben, Simeon, Levi and Judah; Issachar, Zebulun and Benjamin; Dan and Naphtali; Gad and Asher. The descendants of Jacob numbered seventy in all; Joseph was already in Egypt. Now Joseph and all his brothers and all that generation died, but the Israelites were fruitful and multiplied greatly and became exceedingly numerous, so that the land was filled with them. (1:1–7)

God took one man and miraculously made a family of him. God then miraculously grew the family into a people. There in a foreign land, under the domination of an evil ruler, this family has become prolific!

> Then a new king, who did not know about Joseph, came to power in Egypt. "Look," he said to his people, "the Israelites have become much too numerous for us." . . . But the more they were oppressed, the more they multiplied and spread; so the Egyptians came to dread the Israelites. . . . So God was kind to the midwives and the people increased and became even more numerous. (1:8–9, 12, 20)

By the time we come to Exodus 12:27, the Israelite men number six hundred thousand; counting women and children, that may have been a people of perhaps two million individuals. Growing from a barren couple to a small family of seventy within three generations was a miracle. But increasing from seventy people to two million people in 430 years was a massive miracle!

There's another principle staring up at us from this third divine step: *No amount of evil can destroy the people God chooses to bless.*

This principle has been proven over and over again throughout the history of God's people. One example is the church in the troubled country of Vietnam. After years of bitter strife, in 1972 South Vietnam finally fell to the Communists from the north. At that time all Western missionaries had either been evacuated or, in some cases, captured and executed. Everyone wondered what would become of the relatively tiny Christian population of one hundred fifty thousand Vietnamese Christians.

For decades it was impossible to obtain reliable reports of the welfare of the church in Vietnam. But finally in 2003 restrictions loosened just enough for reliable data to be obtained. The news was nothing short of a miracle. Instead of having been obliterated by the persecution of the Communist rulers, that tiny Christian population of one hundred fifty thousand believers, in a period of just over thirty years, had grown to a church comprised of 1.2 million Christians!

The principle held true for God's people in Egypt of old. Not even Pharaoh's plot to destroy Israel through infanticide stopped God's purpose through His people (1:15–22). It is true: no amount of evil can destroy the people God chooses to bless. God is building His church, and the gates of hell cannot prevail against it (Matt. 16:18).

Step #4: A Leader (Exodus 2–19)

Check the progress so far: one man has become one family which has become a great people. But is this a nation? Not exactly. The label just doesn't legitimately apply yet.

So what is still needed for this throng of people to be considered a nation? Several things, but perhaps first they need a leader.

What is the very next word God speaks to us? "Now a man of the house of Levi married a Levite woman, and she became pregnant and gave birth to a son. When she saw that he was a fine child, she hid him for three months" (Exod. 2:1–2).

Of all the many Hebrew children born at the time, God narrows the focus of His spotlight on center stage in order to tell us the story of just one of them. Why? Because God was giving His growing people the leader they needed!

While many other Hebrew baby boys were murdered (1:15–22), Moses was miraculously preserved for God's purposes (2:1–10). He had been trained in Egypt, but he possessed the heart of a Hebrew! He knew that slavery was not the ultimate goal of God's plan for His people. He knew early on that he had been chosen to deliver God's people—but first he had to be honed and refined for his role.

What do we have thus far? A throng of people. And someone called, willing and refined to lead them. Let's ask the question again, are they a nation yet? No! They cannot be considered a nation because they are slaves! So if they are to become the great nation God promised, what do they need now? Deliverance!

It should come as no surprise then that at this juncture God calls Moses to go to Pharaoh and declare, "Let my people go!" (5:1; 7:16; 8:1, 20–21; 9:1, 13; 10:3–4). You may know of the great struggle as Pharaoh repeatedly hardened his heart toward God. Pharaoh's stubbornness resulted in the famous ten plagues of Egypt (Exod. 7–11) in which the glorious supremacy of God was demonstrated over the false gods of Egypt. The final plague before Israel's deliverance from Egypt was the Passover (Exod. 12), which, while a judgment upon Egypt, was an act of grace to Israel and has become a beautiful picture of God's grace to all people. At the cross, "Christ our Passover lamb [was] sacrificed"

(1 Cor. 5:7) so that we may have relationship with God and so that He may grant us a place within His story.

Have you noticed that God is taking pains at every step of this journey to remind us that everything about everything is *about* the glory of God and *by* the grace of God? As Moses leads the people, we read one account after another of God's glory and grace being demonstrated on behalf of His people, whether it is the powerful deliverance at the Red Sea (Exod. 13–14), the provision of manna and quail in the wilderness (Exod. 16) or water from a rock in a dry and thirsty place (Exod. 17). And even after Moses is lifted up and in place, God continues refining His leader. Exodus 18 tells the story of Jethro, Moses' father-in-law, counseling Moses on delegation.

So here is another principle we do well to mark and remember: *When God wants to make a great people, He forges for Himself a great leader.* Is it possible that much of what is going on in your life right now is happening because God is preparing you for or refining you in the midst of a leadership assignment? It may be that God has more to accomplish through you than your present maturity and competence permit. We generally grow through stressful, difficult seasons when we must lean upon and learn from the Lord. If things are tough right now, it may just be that God is growing you for greater fruitfulness as a leader!

Once again, let's check our progress: God has taken one man and made of him one family numbering seventy people. This family has become a teeming mass of humanity, a unique and distinct people. God has also raised up a leader for this people and delivered them from slavery in Egypt. So what else is needed before we can legitimately call this people a great nation?

Step #5: A Culture (Exodus 20–Deuteronomy)

The Israelites need several things at this point—but perhaps first they need to become a distinct, unique people. They are now out from under the domination of Pharaoh, out of Egypt and in the wilderness of Sinai. Take a second look at this mass of humanity. What do you see? For all of God's glorious and gracious acts on their behalf, they are still a desperately needy people. Upon closer inspection you will notice that they have been captive their entire lives—in fact, for generations. They have been told what to do, when to do it and how to do it for so long that they don't have the foggiest notion about how to live in freedom!

This phenomenon is true also on the personal level. Those who work in the prison system know that people who have been incarcerated often struggle when they attempt to reintegrate with society outside of prison. Their lives have been controlled and directed by others for so long that they often struggle when a myriad of daily decisions are suddenly thrust upon them in what most would call normal, everyday life. Living in freedom is not as easy as one might think!

How then can this newly freed people live personally before God and collectively with one another in such a way that it demonstrates the glory of God and extends the grace of God? They must become a whole new people; they need an entirely different culture.[1]

To this point in our journey through Scripture, things have moved along briskly. Honestly, it's exciting to read about all God did! But something happens along about the middle of the book of Exodus, doesn't it? As you read through your Bible, suddenly the material changes and the pace of your reading slows down. If you are honest, right about here your interest level wanes. You might even scratch your head and ask, what is this all about! Relax. This is the place where people who set out to read through the Bible often slow down. Some even abandon the pursuit altogether and close their Bible because they feel lost and confused.

Therefore, let's pause and assess our progress and take some readings about our present location. Ask yourself, what do I find next in the scriptural record? The answer becomes clear if we stand far enough back to see with some perspective. What we now encounter is the Law of God. Beginning in Exodus 20 and running through the end of Deuteronomy, we encounter the Torah, or what we might more commonly refer to as the Law.

It all begins where we find God giving Moses the Ten Commandments. From there we read not exciting stories of God's deliverance or intervention on behalf of His people but, for the most part, legal statutes. We encounter the moral law of God (like the Ten Commandments), the civil law of God (such as how to handle disagreements, how to live together as neighbors, etc.) and the ceremonial law of God (such as how to worship God, how to offer sacrifices, etc.).

Why the Law? It was, of course, given to show the Israelites how to live with God and with other people. OK, but I ask again, why the Law? The Law was given because this newly freed people required a new culture in order to become the great nation God destined them to be.

Let me add just a word of perspective here. When Jesus came, He came not to abolish the Law, but to fulfill it (Matt. 5:17). Jesus perfectly lived out the moral law of God on our behalf. He also made clear that the civil and ceremonial law are not to hold sway in the church (Mark 7:19; Acts 10:15). Paul makes clear that the Law was never intended as a ladder by which one might climb to heaven through perfect obedience. It was rather to serve as a mirror, showing us our inability to obey God perfectly. Salvation is, and always has been, not by law-doing but by trusting in God's gracious substitute for our sins—Jesus.

For this reason there is often great debate among God's people today about the role of the Law. While we can't take enough space here to answer this question fully, I urge you to notice this: the very giving of the Law was an act of grace. For that newly freed, teeming mass of people in the wilderness to become a nation, they needed to know how to live for God and with one another. The Law is a revelation of God's character. It is an expression of how living in the presence of and for the purpose of this God would look in the details of life.

So even today we each need to know and appreciate this next principle: *God's commands and prohibitions are gracious expressions of His desire that we live in fellowship with Him and for His glory.* When God prohibits something, it is because He wants to give you something better. When God commands something, it is because He is waiting one step of obedience away, ready to reveal more of Himself to you than you could know in the place you are at present.

Progress check! We've got a man, now grown into a family. That family has been miraculously multiplied into a people, a people with a divinely called leader who has led them out of slavery and through whom God has communicated to them a new culture. What else is needed for them to become a great nation?

Step #6: A Land (Joshua, Judges, Ruth)

Quite simply: these people need a place to call home! They need a land of their own.

The first five books of the Bible are called the Pentateuch, or the books (or Law) of Moses. The fifth of these books is Deuteronomy. This English title means "repetition of the law." It arose from a mistranslation of a phrase in Deuteronomy 17:18 ("copy of this law") when the Hebrew manuscripts were translated into Greek several centuries before Christ. This understanding of the word was then carried into the Latin Vulgate. Despite the troubled history behind this title, it is instructive about the contents of this book of the Bible.

Why then a repetition of God's Law? It was, quite simply, because entirely new generations of Israelites were sitting on the bank of the Jordan River, opposite the land God had promised to them. They were poised to rise and enter in. God had promised this land to Abraham, though He had told him there would be a four-hundred-year delay before they could take possession of the land (Gen. 15:13–16). Allowing that period of waiting was a gracious act of God toward the unrepentant people who filled the land before Israel came to claim it (15:16). But now that period of gracious patience had passed.

The people positioned on the banks of the Jordan are peering across at the land they'd so longed for. They are no longer a family; they are a great people with a new culture. They are poised to become a nation. Their transformation from being a single individual to a vast people has not been a smooth one; and having become a people, they have not traveled a straight line from Mount Sinai to the Promised Land.

A generation before, Moses had led their fathers to the fringe of the Promised Land. Moses had exhorted that first generation to go in by faith, to conquer the peoples dwelling there and possess the land for themselves. At that time God had instructed Moses to send twelve men in to spy out the land (Num. 13:3–16). In their report ten of the twelve testified that it was indeed a great land but that it was filled with scary people (13:27–30)! The two remaining spies, however, believed that God could enable them to conquer and possess the land which He had promised to them.

One of these two, Caleb, declared, "We should go up and take possession of the land, for we can certainly do it" (13:30). Unfortunately, "the men who had gone up with him said, 'We can't attack those people; they are stronger than we are'" (13:31). What is more, "they spread among the Israelites a bad report about the land they had explored. They said, 'The land we explored devours those living in it. All the people we saw there are of great size'" (13:32).

Unbelief takes root more quickly in human nature than triumphant faith does, so we should not be surprised to learn that the greater percentage voted with the rebels and refused to obey God's command (Num. 14). In the face of their rebellion, God threatened to destroy the people and to begin again with just one man, this time with Moses (14:12). Think of it! Moses could have been the new Abraham! But Moses, in his meekness, instead of going for personal glory and grace, interceded on behalf of the people. And God responded with these words:

> I have forgiven them, as you asked. Nevertheless, *as surely as I live and as surely as the glory of the* LORD *fills the whole earth* [note God's repetition of His ultimate goal!], not one of the men who saw my glory and the miraculous signs I performed in Egypt and in the desert but who disobeyed me and tested me ten times— not one of them will ever see the land I promised on oath to their forefathers. No one who has treated me with contempt will ever see it." (14:20–23)

God promptly turned that generation around and guided them back into the wilderness. They spent the next forty years in that desert, wandering until that entire generation passed away (except Caleb and Joshua).

Again, there is an enduring principle we need to note: *God's work will be done. Your disobedience won't stop Him; it only determines your participation in His grace and glory.* Has God called you to a bold step of faith? Does that frighten you? Are you having second thoughts about obeying Him? Prayerfully reread this principle!

This brings us back to the next generation of people, sitting on the muddy banks of the Jordan River—and to the reason that Moses restates and reapplies God's Law (Deuteronomy). This new generation needs to understand and enter into the new culture God intends them to live in while in the Promised Land that lies before them. They had not been at Mount Sinai, or at least had not been of an age to fully appreciate the revelation that had taken place there.

Having restated the Law, Moses climbed the slopes of Mount Nebo, and God gave him a glimpse of the land which he had so long dreamed of and pursued (Deut. 34:1–4). There Moses died and was buried by God's own hand (34:5–6).

Quite a story! Only one problem: Aren't we regressing? We just lost the leader that was required for the plan to unfold! And we observe no progress toward actually possessing the land! Who is going to step into the leadership vacuum created by Moses' death? Who will lead the charge to go into Canaan and take possession of the land promised to them? By God's design, Moses had groomed Joshua for just this position and purpose (34:9).

Turn the last page of the book of Deuteronomy. What greets you on the next page? The title "Joshua"! As the book of Joshua opens, we discover the people of Israel going in and taking the land God has promised them. The book of Joshua is relatively simple to understand. It is divided neatly in two: the land conquered (Josh. 1–12) and the land divided (Josh. 13–21). The book that bears Joshua's name describes about 350 years of Israelite history. And this is some of the most exciting reading in all of the Old Testament! But due to the purpose and pace of our journey, I can't recount all of it for you here.

Having swiftly arrived at the final chapter of Joshua, let's stop and take a reading on our progress toward the building of this one great nation. How are we doing? As we move into the book of Judges, it becomes painfully apparent things aren't going well at all. As we start to read, you are liable to ask, what has happened here? The excitement of Joshua turns to the horrors of Judges! In the pages of Judges we read horrible stories of, among other things, gross sexual immorality, murder and even dismemberment!

It's enough to make a person wonder aloud, "This stuff is in the Bible! What's going on here?"

Good question. Here's the heart of it—the people of God no longer had a central leader. Joshua and his entire generation had now passed away. "Israel served the LORD throughout the lifetime of Joshua and of the elders who outlived him and who had experienced everything the LORD had done for Israel" (Josh.

24:31). But when "that whole generation had been gathered to their fathers, another generation grew up, who knew neither the LORD nor what he had done for Israel" (Judg. 2:10).

This lack of enduring central leadership kept the people from obeying God's command to fully possess the land and gave way to atrocious moral pendulum swings: the people alternated between utter rebellion and selfishness to repentant prayers for help after seasons of divine discipline.

In response to these prayers for mercy, God raised up judges to deliver the people. The judges were basically regional heroes who rallied God's people back to Him and His purposes. Yet as soon as God extended His grace or demonstrated His glory in response to His people's repentance, they resorted once again to their sinful pursuits. The entire era of the judges is described by an oft repeated phrase found throughout the book of Judges: "The Israelites did evil in the eyes of the LORD" (2:11; 3:7, 12; 4:1; 6:1; 10:6; 13:1). Perhaps this is the classic statement explaining the source of their problems: "In those days there was no king in Israel. Everyone did what was right in his own eyes" (17:6, ESV; see also 21:25).

Here we have a vast people who have been given God's revelation and who live in a land of their own—but they are not a nation, they are a lawless mob! They need a central ruler.

It is so often true that just when things look darkest, God sends a ray of light to cheer our hearts, reminding us that He is still on His throne and that His plan has not been thwarted. We can see this when we turn the last page of Judges. There we find the short little book of Ruth.

Many read Ruth as a romantic tale of God's protection of a disheartened woman and her daughter-in-law. While it is that, there is a more strategic message to it. This little book tells us that "the king is coming!" In the dark days of the judges (Ruth 1:1), God was quietly, faithfully working out His eternal purposes. The entire story of Ruth was unfolded to show us that

God was drawing a straight line through the darkness to the light of Israel's greatest king—David (4:16–17).

The overarching story being told in Joshua, Judges and Ruth concerns the quest to fully possess the land of Canaan, but along the way God has been preparing us for the next step in our journey.

Look at God's inspired segue in this unfolding drama: one man—a family—a people—a leader—a culture—a land—and next . . . a king!

Step #7: A King (1 Samuel–1 Kings 10)

As we search the Scripture from First Samuel through First Kings, looking for a suitable king, we discover that four personalities dominate the landscape of these pages of Scripture.

The first is Samuel. His story is recounted in First Samuel 1–7. Samuel was a bit of a transitional character. He was the last of the judges, but he was also a prophet and a priest. As remarkable and irreplaceable as Samuel was, he was not the one to fill the office of king—that post was still empty. Samuel was a bridge. As the last of the judges, he oversaw the transition to an established, human king over Israel. He anointed the first king of Israel.

God had said all along that He would raise up a king for His nation: "When you enter the land the LORD your God is giving you and have taken possession of it and settled in it, and you say, 'Let us set a king over us like all the nations around us,' be sure to appoint over you the king the LORD your God chooses" (Deut. 17:14–15). This is precisely what transpired:

> So all the elders of Israel gathered together and came to Samuel at Ramah. They said to him, "You are old, and your sons do not walk in your ways; now appoint a king to lead us, such as all the other nations have." But when they said, "Give us a king to lead us," this displeased Samuel; so he prayed to the LORD. And the LORD told him: "Listen to all that the people

are saying to you; it is not you they have rejected, but they have rejected me as their king." (1 Sam. 8:4–7)

God did not intend to reign over the nation in a theocratic government of direct rule, but He extended His rule over them through a man. It was not Israel's request for a king that was misguided; it was the motive behind their request. They wanted to be just like *all the other nations!* But they were not just like any other nation, and their desire sounds an ominous minor key from the orchestra pit. A sense of foreboding washes over us, almost as a prophetic warning of difficult days ahead. Yet Samuel obeyed God, and God led him to Saul.

Saul is the second major personality to dominate the stage during this part of the scene (1 Sam. 9–31). Saul was selected and anointed as Israel's first king. He seemed as though he was everything a king should be, but soon enough we discover that Saul was not set on the same goal that God was. His reign did not last long, and it ended portentously.

David, the third personality, now enters the scene. Once on stage, he does not exit for long time (1 Sam. 13–2 Sam. 31). His personality dominates; his singular blessing by God is breathtaking. God, in His grace, makes David the great king of Israel! To David God promised, "Your house and your kingdom will endure forever before me; your throne will be established forever" (2 Sam. 7:16). This is grace!

But as is always the case, human beings, even greatly blessed ones, die. David eventually passes from the scene, and the last great personality to grace the stage during this portion of God's drama is David's son Solomon (1 Kings 1–10). Through Solomon's reign Israel finally had peace. Her borders were established. Her infrastructure was built up. From the beginning Solomon displayed wise leadership. He was appointed by God to fulfill his father's dream—building a temple for God in Jerusalem!

It is time to check our progress once again. Are we now looking upon a nation? Yes! But, if I may forestall the balloons, confetti and party hats for just a moment, may I ask, do we have a *great* nation?

That would seem a difficult question to answer. How would one discern the difference between a nation and a *great* nation? Perhaps we should return to our two fixed constants, glory and grace. What do they tell us?

Begin with grace. With Solomon front and center, do we find evidences of God's grace being uniquely and strategically extended? Indeed we do! Early on in Solomon's reign we read that "the LORD appeared to Solomon during the night in a dream, and God said, 'Ask for whatever you want me to give you'" (1 Kings 3:5). Imagine! What grace!

Solomon's reply? "Give me wisdom!" (3:6–9). God's response to such a request in the face of unparalleled grace was to give Solomon what he requested and much, much more (3:10–14)! There must never be any doubt; God is utterly committed to extending grace to His people!

So herein lays another principle that endures through all the ages: *God's kingdom is advanced when those in authority are committed to living for God's glory and by God's grace.*

But this is only one of our two fixed constants. If we are to get an accurate reading, we must look not only for grace, but for a demonstration of God's glory as well.

So take a deep breath; we are about to reach the dramatic climax of Act I. Not just of Act I, Scene 1, but of the whole of Act I! We will not behold a revelation of God's glory to surpass what we are about to see until the curtain opens on Act II.

We have seen God move from one man, to one family, to a vast people, to a great leader, to a new culture, in a promised land, with an anointed king to whom God is extending His grace in unprecedented ways. We finally have a nation! But something more is needed for it to be the great nation God promised.

Step #8: A Temple (1 Kings 5–8)

The final step in the formation of this great nation is seen when God has a temple to dwell in.

A temple? Why a temple?

David dreamed of building a temple in which God would continually manifest His glory. But God determined that this privilege would await David's son Solomon. Thus, we are not surprised to observe Solomon deploying Israel's vast resources—which God has extended to this new nation by His grace—toward the preparation and completion of the glorious temple of Jerusalem (1 Kings 5–7). When finally the temple is ready, Solomon prepares to dedicate the building to the Lord (1 Kings 8). The Ark of the Covenant is carefully brought into the newly prepared temple. "When the priests withdrew from the Holy Place, the cloud filled the temple of the LORD. And the priests could not perform their service because of the cloud, *for the glory of the LORD filled his temple*" (8:10–11)!

Do you see? We have a front row seat as the glory of God comes to abide with His people. We are looking on as God's grace is extended in unprecedented ways and His glory displayed in unparalleled terms!

Lean back. Catch your breath. And as you do, note this final abiding principle: *God is unreservedly committed to displaying His glory and extending His grace!* You can count on this. It is always, always true, no matter where you find yourself in the journey from eternity past to eternity future.

Remember, the purpose of Act I, Scene 1 was to use one man (Abraham) to build one great nation (Israel) through whom God will provide the one Savior (Jesus) who will reveal God's glory and extend God's grace to all people.

Have we made progress? Yes! Absolutely, yes!

We have looked on as God led us from creation to the Fall and on toward His promised redemption. To bring about this redemption, God has moved events along, starting with a man, then building to a family, a people, a leader, a culture, a land, a king . . . and all of it by His grace and for His glory!

May I ask, are you depending upon God's grace? Are you depending upon His grace for the problems you face, the relationships you share in, the needs you have? Are you committed to glorifying God in every situation, no matter what it costs you? Then rest assured that your story will matter!

Writing Your Story

As you prepare to move on to the next scene in this divine drama, stop and consider how what we've found here in Act I, Scene 1 helps you write your God-intended story. Fill in the blanks below with the eight principles we have discovered. Pray over each one, making them a matter of thoughtful communion with God. Ask Him to show you how each principle applies to your life. Note any thoughts He gives you along with any steps of surrender and/or obedience He directs you to.

1. When God wants to do a great thing, He graces

   _____ person that He might grace _____

   _____ people.

2. God never loses track of His _____ and works

   even in our darkest hours, so He can redeem them and

   fulfill His good _____ through us.

3. No amount of evil can destroy the people God chooses to

   _____.

4. When God wants to make a great people, He will forge for

   Himself a great _____.

5. God's _____ and _____ are
    gracious expressions of His desire that we live in fellowship
    with Him and for His glory.

6. God's work will be done; your _____ won't
    stop Him, it will only determine your participation in His
    grace and glory.

7. God's kingdom is advanced when leaders are commit-
    ted to living for God's _____ and by God's
    _____.

8. God is unreservedly _____ to displaying His
    glory and extending His grace!

Reviewing God's Story

Take a moment before you move on and review what we've
learned thus far about God's eternal purposes. Force the answers
from your brain, down your arm and through the pencil in your
hand!

God's plan is to use one man (_____) to build one
great nation (_____) through whom He will provide the one Savior (_____) who will reveal God's glory
and extend God's grace to all people.

Now record the eight steps God takes as He works to inau-
gurate this plan (Act I, Scene 1). Be sure to record the section
of Scripture which describes each step.

1. _____ (_____)

2. _____ (_____)

3. _____ (_____)

4. _____ (_____)

5. _____ (_____)

6. _____ (_____)

7. _____ (_____)

8. _____ (_____)

Remembering God's Story

Scriptures	Genesis 12–1 Kings 10

Key Characters	Abraham, Isaac, Jacob, Joseph, Moses, the Judges, Samuel, Saul, David and Jonathan

Key Events	Abraham chosen, Joseph preserved, Israelites in Egypt, Red Sea, Exodus, Promised Land, the Judges, a king given, David's reign, Solomon's temple, God's glory

Key Verses	"The LORD did not set his affection on you and choose you because you were more numerous than other peoples, for you were the fewest of all peoples. But it was because the LORD loved you and kept the oath he swore to your forefathers." Deuteronomy 7:7–8

Eternity Past

← Creation

← Fall / Flood / Babel   } Gen. 1–11

← Abraham–Joseph

← Moses & the Exodus

← Rebellion & wandering

← Promised Land   Gen. 12–
                                              1 Kings 10
← Judges & Samuel

← 1st King: Saul

← David's reign

← Solomon & Temple ⚡ GLORY!

2,000 yrs.

God's Story

Eternity Future

ACT 1, SCENE 2

A Weeping Grace
1 Kings 11–2 Chronicles, the Prophets

What does it take to make you cry? Loss? Joy? Onions? Tears may come for any number of reasons. It's quite possible one of those occasions has paid you a visit recently. Even as I write, I'm reminded that my life is filled with people who find themselves in a season of weeping. For some it is caused by the pain of "the valley of the shadow of death." For others it is because of unspeakable joy—delight so intense that it demands expression and presses itself out of the corners of their eyes. For others it is the result of frustration. Maybe even for a few, it's because of onions.

Nobody I know seeks to weep. It's embarrassing. It's exhausting. It breeds feelings of vulnerability. Those salty, acrid tears are unwelcome visitors. Yet maybe you find yourself weeping these days.

Whatever the cause, you wonder: *How have all my hopes for the future crumbled into so much pain?*

God hears your question. He sees your tears. In fact, the Bible says God catches every one of them and keeps them in a bottle (Ps. 56:8). But He does more than just hear your questions and record the number of your tears. God *feels* your pain. It is true. God feels your pain, for He has lived in it for years.

As we trace God's story, we are discovering that history is

a drama—and one that is full of drama! We have just followed eight divine strides of progress through the passing of some two thousand years. It was a period of triumphant advance en route to the fulfillment of God's one plan. When the curtain dropped at the end of that time, Solomon was on the throne, receiving unprecedented grace from God (since he was given a blank check by God) and beholding unprecedented demonstrations of His glory (since God filled the temple Solomon had built).

God's purpose in choosing one man to build this one nation was that God might through that nation bring one great Savior (Jesus)—through whom God's grace might be extended and His glory demonstrated to all creation. We've become accustomed to remarkable progress in the divine pursuit of His plan. In fact, as we come now to Act I, Scene 2, we expect more quick advances. But instead, what we observe are tears—divine tears. What we hear is weeping—heavenly weeping. Unfortunately, the drama is now racked by the introduction of significant conflict. Whereas earlier we saw a spurned grace transformed into a pursuing grace, we behold now a weeping grace.

In terms of the pages in your Bible, this scene extends from First Kings 11 through the end of Second Chronicles, and it also encompasses most of the prophets. In terms of years on the calendar, it covers nearly four hundred years. Are you ready to walk a forty-decade trail of tears?

Research reveals that the chemical composition of tears differs depending upon what generates them. Tears of grief or sadness have a different chemical makeup than tears of irritation (such as from onions or dust), lubrication (for normal eye health) or even joy. Researchers have discovered that tears of grief have more cortisal, a hormone released in the body during times of stress. A crying jag may be your body's effort at ridding itself of toxins!

In the scene that is about to be played out before us, we discover that God's tears were evoked by deep grief. In the face of unparalleled expressions of grace and glory, God was spurned and His heart rent. As the curtain opens once again, see if you can detect the components that make up the tears of God. You'll discover five elements that contribute to the composition of these divine tears.

Adultery

Long before God granted Israel's request for a king, He predicted that they would one day be ruled by one. God prescribed beforehand how that king was to behave: "The king, moreover, must not acquire great numbers of horses for himself or make the people return to Egypt to get more of them, for the LORD has told you, 'You are not to go back that way again.' He must not take many wives, or his heart will be led astray. He must not accumulate large amounts of silver and gold" (Deut. 17:16–17). It was in precisely these ways that Solomon then failed the Lord.

Did you note, just before the curtain closed on Act I, Scene 1, how Solomon and his kingdom were described? God lifted Solomon up, and that young man made for himself a kingdom of unparalleled splendor (1 Kings 10:14–29). As king, he multiplied horses (10:26), even sending to Egypt for them (10:28–29). God said that Israel's king "must not take many wives" (Deut. 17:17), yet listen to the first words to arise from the stage in Act I, Scene 2:

> King Solomon, however, loved many foreign women besides Pharaoh's daughter—Moabites, Ammonites, Edomites, Sidonians and Hittites. They were from nations about which the LORD had told the Israelites, "You must not intermarry with them, because they will surely turn your hearts after their gods." Nevertheless, Solomon held fast to them in love. He had seven hundred wives of royal birth and three hundred concubines, and his wives led him astray. As Solomon grew old, his wives turned his heart after other gods, and his heart was not fully devoted to the LORD his God, as the heart of

David his father had been. He followed Ashtoreth the goddess of the Sidonians, and Molech the detestable god of the
Ammonites. So Solomon did evil in the eyes of the LORD; he
did not follow the LORD completely, as David his father had
done. On a hill east of Jerusalem, Solomon built a high place
for Chemosh the detestable god of Moab, and for Molech the
detestable god of the Ammonites. He did the same for all his
foreign wives, who burned incense and offered sacrifices to
their gods. (1 Kings 11:1–8)

David had been a man after God's own heart, but now something clearly has changed! David failed the Lord in many ways,
but, when confronted with God's will, he chose God's way (see
Ps. 32, 38, 51). And despite his other sinful choices, he never left
God for other gods! Solomon, conversely, went after many gods,
even after God had expressly told him not to do so (1 Kings 9:6;
2 Chron. 7:19–22).

Cup your hand behind your ear and make sure you hear
well God's response to Solomon's unfaithfulness.

The LORD became angry with Solomon because his heart had
turned away from the LORD, the God of Israel, who had appeared to him twice. Although he had forbidden Solomon to
follow other gods, Solomon did not keep the LORD's command. So the LORD said to Solomon, "Since this is your attitude and you have not kept my covenant and my decrees,
which I commanded you, I will most certainly tear the kingdom away from you and give it to one of your subordinates."
(1 Kings 11:9–11)

We're only moments into this second scene, and already the
entire plan—which has been worked out now for two thousand
years—has come to a screeching halt!

Idolatry plagued Israel throughout its history. Sometimes we
shake our heads at how frequently they fell into the same trap. If
we are honest, however, idolatry is a threat to us as well. You've

not necessarily passed the idolatry test just because you haven't fashioned a physical image and paid homage before it.

The New Testament warns us against the idolatry of our appetites ("Their god is their stomach," Phil. 3:19), materialism ("Greed . . . is idolatry," Col. 3:5), and immorality (An "immoral . . . person . . . is an idolater," Eph. 5:5). We fashion gods in the workshop of the mind. We take up the name of the true God, but import to it characteristics foreign to His nature. We style a safe god, a controllable god—one whose measure we have taken, whose rough spots we have conveniently smoothed and whose dangers we have tamed. In such cases we worship a false god, a caricature of God. Little wonder the apostle John warned us, "Little children, guard yourselves from idols" (1 John 5:21, NASB).

As we break down the makeup of God's tears, are there any lessons we might glean and apply in the search for our own story? Indeed there are. Try this one on for size: *You only find your place in God's plan as you remain faithful to the God who loves you.* In a few moments I'm going to encourage you to sit before God and invite Him to expose any rivals for His affection. But for now, let me ask, what has become of God's plan? What of those two thousand years of progress? What of the great nation promised to Abraham, which was to be the channel for the Messiah?

Grace

What we behold next is another, even more remarkable, expression of grace. The unfaithfulness of God's people generates another component in the chemical makeup of the divine tears.

In the face of the spiritual adultery we have just witnessed, God extends a double grace. The first wave of God's grace is seen in His commitment to be faithful to the promises He had given to David. Even as He disciplines the people, God states that Solomon's line would retain one tribe, Judah (with Benjamin they would make up the southern kingdom of Judah), and thus the lineage of the Messiah:

About that time Jeroboam was going out of Jerusalem, and
Ahijah the prophet of Shiloh met him on the way, wearing a
new cloak. The two of them were alone out in the country,
and Ahijah took hold of the new cloak he was wearing and
tore it into twelve pieces. Then he said to Jeroboam, "Take ten
pieces for yourself, for this is what the LORD, the God of Israel, says: 'See, I am going to tear the kingdom out of Solomon's
hand and give you ten tribes. But for the sake of my servant
David and the city of Jerusalem, which I have chosen out of
all the tribes of Israel, he will have one tribe. I will do this
because they have forsaken me and worshiped Ashtoreth the
goddess of the Sidonians, Chemosh the god of the Moabites,
and Molech the god of the Ammonites, and have not walked
in my ways, nor done what is right in my eyes, nor kept my
statutes and laws as David, Solomon's father, did. But I will
not take the whole kingdom out of Solomon's hand; I have
made him ruler all the days of his life for the sake of David my
servant, whom I chose and who observed my commands and
statutes. I will take the kingdom from his son's hands and give
you ten tribes. I will give one tribe to his son so that David
my servant may always have a lamp before me in Jerusalem,
the city where I chose to put my Name. (1 Kings 11:29–36)

The second wave of divine grace washes over us as we see
that, though Judah would retain the hope of the Davidic line,
God nevertheless offered Jeroboam, who had been one of Solomon's officials, the opportunity to become a great nation in his
own right (the northern kingdom of Israel)!

However, as for you, I will take you, and you will rule over all
that your heart desires; you will be king over Israel. If you do
whatever I command you and walk in my ways and do what
is right in my eyes by keeping my statutes and commands, as
David my servant did, I will be with you. I will build you a
dynasty as enduring as the one I built for David and will give
Israel to you. I will humble David's descendants because of
this, but not forever.'" (11:37–39)

What do we make of this? There are many lessons to be learned here, but know at least this much—God is more ready to extend grace to you than you can ever know.

In the face of a double dose of divine grace, how did the people respond? With a double rebellion! Solomon's son Rehoboam, given the opportunity to become king in his father's place, rejected God's purpose by proving a hardhearted, harsh dictator (12:1–19). This was matched by a full-fledged, in-your-face flouting by Jeroboam of the remarkable grace of God extended to him (12:20–33).

To be honest, Jeroboam was in a tough spot. The temple, along with all its sacrifices and worship opportunities, was located in the southern kingdom of Judah. All members of Israel were duty bound to go up to the temple three times a year for the annual feasts, lest they be found unfaithful to God. It is easy to see why Jeroboam would be uneasy with such an arrangement—it could appear to threaten his newly acquired kingdom!

But instead of going the way of faith and humility, Jeroboam schemed and plotted. He declared to his new subjects, "It is too much for you to go up to Jerusalem" (12:28). The man-who-would-be-king crafted for his people a religion of convenience. He provided convenient gods (two golden calves, 12:28) who were served at convenient altars (at Dan and Bethel, 12:29) by a convenient priesthood (12:31) with a convenient schedule of worship (12:32–33).

In the face of a double grace came a double rebellion. What can we learn about our own story here? At least this much: *You only find your place in God's plan as you embrace the grace He extends to you.* God has extended His grace to you in Christ. He has delivered over to you a copy of His Holy Scriptures. He has given you His Holy Spirit, the Author of the Book, in order to guide you into the fullness of His grace and the extension of His glory. But somewhere along the way you are heard to complain,

"This is hard! No one told me it would be this difficult! I don't think I want to do this anymore!"

Take a deep breath. Be still. That spirit within you is the same one which long ago forged a religion of convenience. Remember, you will only find your place in God's plan as you embrace the grace He extends to you.

Grief

Following Israel's rebellion, a third element is discovered in the makeup of divine tears. This substance only heightens the salty bitterness of those tears.

We encounter grief every week. Lost jobs, lost fortunes, lost dreams, lost loved ones. We know how bitter tears of sorrow can be. But what does divine grief look like? We are given a glimpse into God's heartache in two ways.

The first profile of divine grief is drawn with the pencil of *history*. So sad is the story that it is told twice—once in First and Second Kings and again in Second Chronicles. Here we trace the story of the kings that followed Rehoboam and Jeroboam. Each kingdom had approximately twenty such rulers throughout their history. The northern kingdom, Israel, never enjoyed a truly good or godly one among their number. Among Israel's kings were men whose reigns were as short as seven days and as long as forty-one years. The southern kingdom of Judah experienced the leadership of a few good and godly kings, but many others were wicked. One of their rulers sat on the throne for only three months, while another reigned for fifty-five years.

Both north and south of their shared border, we observe a swirling vortex of downward moral descent. This is the view the facts, figures, dates and names give to us. This is the tangible kingdom that could be seen, touched and watched. But there is another way we can taste this grief. It is to hear it rather than simply observe it.

The second sketch of divine grief is drawn with the stylus

of *prophecy*. The ministry of prophecy among God's people had begun with Moses. Samuel also had filled such a role. But with the division of the kingdom, the role of the prophets became much more prominent. The prophets allow us to hear God's heart, listen to His sobs, taste His tears: "Oh, that my head were a spring of water and my eyes a fountain of tears! I would weep day and night for the slain of my people" (Jer. 9:1). "Oh, how can I give you up, Israel? How can I let you go? . . . My heart is torn within me, and my compassion overflows" (Hos. 11:8, NLT). "Turn away from me; let me weep bitterly. Do not try to console me over the destruction of my people" (Isa. 22:4).

Do you hear? Do you taste the acrid tears? These are the tears of a *Father* weeping over a prodigal child: "These are rebellious people, deceitful children, children unwilling to listen to the LORD's instruction" (Isa. 30:9). These are the tears of a *Husband* weeping over an adulterous wife: "The LORD said to me, 'Go, show your love to your wife again, though she is loved by another and is an adulteress. Love her as the LORD loves the Israelites, though they turn to other gods and love the sacred raisin cakes'" (Hos. 3:1). These are the tears of a *Shepherd* weeping over a wayward flock: "But if you do not listen, I will weep in secret because of your pride; my eyes will weep bitterly, overflowing with tears, because the LORD's flock will be taken captive" (Jer. 13:17).

Are you familiar with the expression "Trail of Tears"? It dates back to 1838 when President Andrew Jackson approved the forced relocation of the Cherokee nation. The death march resulted in some four thousand Cherokees perishing en route to their new "home." So characteristic was this kind of treatment toward other Native American people that the expression has become descriptive of their sufferings as well.

To be sure, there were many tears among the people of Judah and Israel during these hard years, and we don't want to downplay their suffering, but this entire portion of Scripture is about the trail of tears falling from God's heart. His heart has broken more times that we can know. He weeps over the failure of His people to embrace His grace and esteem His glory.

But let's be honest, this is more than a history lesson; this is a personal lesson (Rom. 15:4; 1 Cor. 10:11). God weeps when I pursue my purposes rather than His; when I live off my own resources, spurning His grace. Know this: *You only find your place in God's plan as you own the grief you cause Him by your sin.* Though He had committed no sin, "during the days of Jesus' life on earth, he offered up prayers and petitions with loud cries and tears to the one who could save him from death, and he was heard because of his reverent submission" (Heb. 5:7). Why? Because sin has a price.

Discipline

Because sin carries a price, one of the elements of God's tears is discipline. Every loving father disciplines his children (Prov. 3:11–12). And He from whom all the lines of fatherhood are drawn can do no less (Heb. 12:5–11).

For this reason, as promised (Deut. 28:63), God used Assyria to bring down the northern kingdom of Israel and to lead them away captive into exile in 722 BC. Though it took a little longer for Him to do it, God similarly used Babylon to destroy Judah and to exile her citizens as well. Judah's demise came in three stages: 606 BC (Daniel and friends among the exiles), 597 BC (the royal treasuries taken) and finally 586 BC (the temple and city destroyed and the walls pulled down).

From this it is clear that God controls the nations and uses them to carry out His purpose. Through Jeremiah He declared, "I will summon all the peoples of the north and my servant Nebuchadnezzar king of Babylon" (25:9). Similarly, He announced, "Now I will hand all your countries over to my servant Nebuchadnezzar king of Babylon" (27:6). Of a prophet who said Nebuchadnezzar would not be victorious over Judah, God said, "You have preached rebellion against the LORD" (28:16).

But how can this be? How can God cast off His people? What about His promises? What about His one great plan?!

OK, take a deep breath. Realize that this discipline did not happen suddenly. Step back from the precipice and you'll notice that during the long years of decline that led to this divine discipline, the prophets were called upon to share God's grief over His people. The pain of those years was enough to crush those to whom God had entrusted His heart. So great was the anguish of watching the spiritual decline of God's people that it moved Habakkuk to cry out, "How long, O LORD?" (1:2). The sin of his people was so extensive that the prophet wondered aloud as to why God did not act!

God was gracious enough to answer the prophet, "I am going to do something in your days that you would not believe, even if you were told" (1:5). But that "something" was that God was going to use the Babylonians to discipline His people Israel! And indeed Habakkuk, and all like him, could scarcely believe the report.

Yet in the midst of the confusion, God took His spokesman, and through him His people, back to the one great plan He had set out from the beginning: "The earth will be filled with the knowledge of the glory of the LORD, as the waters cover the sea" (2:14).

The prophet, seeing that God can't always be figured out but He can be trusted, closed his prophecy with a magnificent prayer of surrender and faith: "Though the fig tree does not bud and there are no grapes on the vines, though the olive crop fails and the fields produce no food, though there are no sheep in the pen and no cattle in the stalls, yet I will rejoice in the LORD, I will be joyful in God my Savior" (3:17–18).

Can you similarly trust God, even though you may not understand all He is doing or allowing in your life at present? Here's another lesson along the way: *You only find your place in*

God's plan as you learn from the discipline He sends. Mark it down.
Make a note of it. You're going to need it sometime, even if not
at the moment.

Separation

Just as God's grief can be traced both historically and pro-
phetically, so too can the separation of God from His people be
viewed from two perspectives. In one sense we will see God actually *thrusting* the people from His presence; in the other we will
observe Him *withdrawing* Himself from their midst.

Having endured rejection again and again and having sent
wave after wave of patient, prophetic grace, God sent His people
from His presence. This was the case when the northern kingdom was taken away to Assyria:

> So the LORD was very angry with Israel and *removed them from
> his presence.* Only the tribe of Judah was left. . . . Therefore the
> LORD rejected all the people of Israel; he afflicted them and
> gave them into the hands of plunderers, until *he thrust them
> from his presence. . . . The LORD removed them from his presence,*
> as he had warned through all his servants the prophets. (2
> Kings 17:18, 20, 23)

God dealt in the same way with the kingdom of Judah: "It
was because of the LORD's anger that all this happened to Jerusalem and Judah, and in the end *he thrust them from his presence*"
(Jer. 52:3).

There was also, however, a very real sense in which God withdrew Himself from the midst of His own. We encounter this
most overwhelming picture in Ezekiel. Before you spread your
fingers wide enough to look between them at the sight about to
befall God's people, take stock of our two constants: God's grace
and God's glory. Do you recall the climactic event which signaled God had indeed built a great nation? It came when God's
glory filled the temple. This was the defining moment which

changed Israel from simply *a* nation into a *great* nation!

Is That a Nod of Your Head?

Good, you remember. Are you ready, then, for what comes next? Peek now between the fingers you slapped over your eyes in your effort to block out the horrors we've been forced to witness.

Ezekiel begins with an overwhelming, almost indescribable picture of God's glory (Ezek. 1:4–28). There was a windstorm, lightning, fire, a brilliant light, creatures beyond description, wheels of unearthly motion and purpose, an overhanging expanse that sparkled like glass, a roar like the sound of rushing waters and a throne that looked as if it were made of sapphire upon which was seated "a figure like that of a man" (1:26). From "what appeared to be his waist up he looked like glowing metal, as if full of fire . . . and brilliant light surrounded him. Like the appearance of a rainbow in the clouds on a rainy day, so was the radiance around him" (1:27–28). "This," explains the prophet, "was the appearance of the likeness of the glory of the LORD" (1:28).

This glorious presence dominates the first portion of Ezekiel's prophecy. Though he speaks of other matters, he repeatedly returns to the likeness of God's glory, as if he can never fully take his eye off Him. But then the prophet details the sad movements as God's glory begins to depart from the midst of His adulterous people.

God's glorious presence normally dwelt *within the Holy of Holies*, inside the heart of the temple itself:

> The Spirit lifted me up between earth and heaven and in visions of God he took me to Jerusalem, to the entrance to the north gate of the inner court, where the idol that provokes to jealousy stood. And there before me was the glory of the God of Israel, as in the vision I had seen in the plain." (8:3–4)

Ezekiel watched God's glory withdraw from the Holy of Holies to *the door of the temple*: "Now the glory of the God of Israel went up from above the cherubim, where it had been, and moved to the threshold of the temple" (9:3). But the Lord did not wait there. He moved out of the temple and to *the gate of the city*: "Then the glory of the LORD departed from over the threshold of the temple and stopped above the cherubim. While I watched, the cherubim spread their wings and rose from the ground, and as they went, the wheels went with them. They stopped at the entrance to the east gate of the LORD's house, and the glory of the God of Israel was above them" (10:18–19). Finally the Lord moved *out of the city* of Jerusalem altogether and was last seen heading east: "The glory of the LORD went up from within the city and stopped above the mountain east of it" (11:23).

This is a good time to fall silent. It's best not to say another word. Take a few moments and simply absorb what has just happened. This is breathtaking! This changes everything! It certainly appears as though God had abandoned His one redemptive channel to bring forth the one Savior of the world . . .

Now, in the stillness and silence, ask yourself: What is God saying to me through this? For now simply let this register: *You only find your place in God's plan as you value His presence more than your plans.*

God weeps, as He did over Israel and Judah, when those who call on His name do not care for His purposes nor carry out His plan. It all begins with *spiritual adultery.* God meets the spiritual adultery with *sacrificial grace.* But if the spiritual adultery is protracted, it produces *sacred grief.* That sacred grief elicits *sympathetic discipline.* If that discipline is unheeded, it creates *spiritual distance.*

Writing Your Story

So what do you do now? Once God's presence departs, is all hope lost? No!

The prophets always preached two great messages: judgment and hope. We'll see more about hope in our next study. But for now, let's jumble the five elements of God's tears which we've just discovered, turning them around so that they may become tears of joy and hope. When you do so, a path of hope will begin to open before your eyes.

First, you must own God's grief over your sins. The Bible calls this confession. This is absolutely necessary, but it is not designed as a final resting place.

Second, you must embrace the grace God is extending to you. This is what the Bible calls faith or trust.

Just because you confess your sins and trust in God's gracious forgiveness through Christ does not mean that all your circumstances will instantly become easy. No; thirdly, you must lean into the discipline of God. This is what discipleship requires. Learn from what you've received from God's hand.

A fourth key step is to constantly renew your commitment to walk in obedience to God. This might also be called consecration.

Finally, determine to value God's presence above all things. That is to say, aim for intimacy with God. God is your very great reward (Gen 15:1; Ps. 142:5; Lam. 3:24). If God is your goal, you can never be foiled!

Now, take a few moments to turn these steps into a season of prayer with God. Don't rush. This is holy work!

- Invite God to share His heart with you—even His grief over your sins.
- Then affirm His promises of forgiveness through Christ. Find some of those promises in the Bible and turn them back to God in prayers of faith.

- Surrender yourself to your heavenly Father, telling Him you want to learn from His discipline.
- Write out a fresh prayer in which you consecrate yourself entirely to God and His purposes.
- Ask God to continue to work in you until you value Him above all else. Invite Him to root out the idols of your life, to remove them and inhabit those places where you've worshiped other gods.

No doubt about it, this has been a painful scene to watch unfold. But there is hope to be found in the drama ahead. For now, allow Wesley L. Duewel to send you off to prayer with this admonition:

> Our world can only be moved Godward by leaders who have shared to a deep degree His heartbreak as He looks in compassion and love on the world. Until you sense the suffering tears in the heart of God, until you share to some extent our Savior's suffering passion in Gethsemane, until you come close enough to God to enable His Spirit to yearn within you with His infinite and unutterable yearning, you are not prepared to minister about the cross.[1]

Reviewing God's Story

1. What five elements are found in God's tears?

   _____

   _____

   _____

   _____

   _____

2. Take a moment to detail the downward spiral of a weeping grace:

    Spiritual _____

    Sacrificial _____

    Sacred _____

    Sympathetic _____

    Spiritual _____

3. Take a moment to complete these principles of application.

    *   You only find your place in God's plan as you remain

        _____ to the God who loves you.

    *   You only find your place in God's plan as you

        _____ the grace He extends to you.

    *   You only find your place in God's plan as you

        _____ the grief you cause Him by your sin.

    *   You only find your place in God's plan as you

        _____ from the discipline He sends.

    *   You only find your place in God's plan as you

        _____ His presence more than your plans.

Remembering God's Story

Scriptures	1 Kings 11–2 Chron., the Prophets
Key Characters	Solomon, Jeroboam, Rehoboam, the kings of Israel and Judah, Elijah, Elisha, the prophets, Nebuchadnezzar
Key Events	Solomon's sin, divided kingdom, declining spirituality, occasional revival, pleading prophets, a weeping God, God's glory departed from the temple!
Key Verses	"The LORD, the God of their fathers, sent word to them through his messengers again and again, because he had pity on his people and on his dwelling place. But they mocked God's messengers, despised his words and scoffed at his prophets until the wrath of the LORD was aroused against his people and there was no remedy." 2 Chronicles 36:15–16

Eternity Past

Creation ⟵ ⎫ Gen. 1–11
Fall / Flood / Babel ⟵ ⎭

The Rise of Israel ⟵ ⎫ Gen. 12–
Temple ⟵ ⚡ **GLORY!** ⎭ 1 Kings 10

Solomon's sin ⟵ ⎫
Divided Kingdom ⟵ ⎪ 1 Kings 11
Failing kings / pleading prophets ⟵ ⎬ –2 Chron.,
Exile! ⟵ ⟶ **GLORY!** ⎪ Prov.
⎭

2,000 yrs.

400 yrs.

God's Story

Eternity Future

ACT 1, SCENE 3

A Faithful Grace
Ezra–Esther, Haggai–Malachi

The end of your strength, your wisdom, your rope . . . your hope. What then? How long can you maintain your grasp on the frayed end of life's tether? Have you ever had to ask, is there a tomorrow for me?

The nation of Israel has come to that place.

When they spurned God's grace (Gen. 1–11), in grace He pursued them (Gen. 12–1 Kings 10). God chose one man to become one great nation to bring one great Savior so that His grace might extend and His glory might be demonstrated to all creation! But even then, that nation rejected His grace. But still again God offered grace—this time a weeping grace (1 Kings 11–Prophets). Finally, after four hundred years of rebellion on the part of Israel, God withdrew. Remember the vision of God's retreat from the temple? Even the infinitely patient God said He'd had enough: "This is what the Sovereign Lord says to the land of Israel: *The end*!" (Ezek. 7:2).

It's frightening enough when you are brought to the end of yourself. But when God is the One who says it's over, it is devastating!

When the curtain fell on Act I, Scene 2, there was nothing left onstage. Jerusalem was destroyed and lay in ruins. The temple was no more. The city's buildings were reduced to charred rubble. Her protective walls had been rolled over into useless piles of stone. We look down on the stage and gaze, as it were, upon a vile, long-past, smoldering ashtray of destruction. There is an old song which lamented, "There's nothing cold as ashes after the fire is gone." Well, the fire of God was gone from Jerusalem! His flaming presence had left the house. The ashes and embers of what once had been were now cold and dead, and the glory years were a distant, painful memory. In exile the Israelites sang dirges like this one:

> By the rivers of Babylon we sat and wept
>   when we remembered Zion.
> There on the poplars
>   we hung our harps,
> for there our captors asked us for songs,
>   our tormentors demanded songs of joy;
>   they said, "Sing us one of the songs of Zion!"
> How can we sing the songs of the LORD
>   while in a foreign land? . . .
> O Daughter of Babylon, doomed to destruction,
>   happy is he who repays you
> for what you have done to us—he who seizes your infants
>   and dashes them against the rocks.
>
> (Ps. 137:1–4, 8–9)

God had made His name to dwell in Jerusalem. Before He withdrew His presence, a person would draw near to God by drawing near to Jerusalem and offering blood sacrifice. What solution was left for sin now? None.

So I ask you, what is left when nothing else is left?

God.

If you had to label what it is about God that makes that answer accurate, what word would you offer? If you put a word to it, what would it be?

Try this: faithful.

What happened to God's plan? What had become of God's decree? To His commitment to redeem us, extending grace and demonstrating glory to all creation through one Savior?

I want you to draw up a chair and observe as Act I, Scene 3 unfolds. As we consider this final scene of Act I, rather than tracing a strict chronology we will observe several principles of God's keeping power. What we will behold is a *faithful grace*. God will reaffirm His purpose, His people and His promise in the concluding years of the Old Testament.

The context of the scene comes from three historical books, Ezra, Nehemiah and Esther, and three prophetic books, Haggai, Zechariah and Malachi, On the calendar this period of time covers about one hundred twenty to one hundred forty years.

We have dubbed this a faithful grace—but faithful to what? At this juncture one might legitimately wonder what is left for God to be faithful to.

God Faithfully Keeps His Purpose

It is a fixed, immutable constant of God's nature: "If we are faithless, he remains faithful, for he cannot disown himself" (2 Tim. 2:13). We are charged not to forget "the unchangeable character of his purpose" (Heb. 6:17, ESV). So don't ever lose sight of God's purpose: God chose one man (Abraham) to build one great nation (Israel) so that through it He might bring one great Savior (Jesus) and thus extend His grace and demonstrate His glory to all creation.

Previously I reminded you that the prophets announced a two-fold message: a message of judgment (discipline), but also one of hope. If we only consider God's judgment and look purely at the brokenness of Israel, heartbroken in exile, then His purpose appears lost. (I stress the word "appears.") But let's look now at the second stream of the prophets' message: hope.

We remember from the previous scene that things were dark in Habakkuk's day. So dark, in fact, that the prophet seemed unable to discern even a ray of hope. Questions breed best in darkness. It's true even for prophets: "How long, O LORD, must I call for help, but you do not listen? . . . Why do you make me look at injustice? Why do you tolerate wrong?" (1:2–3). In essence, Habakkuk cried out as we all have at times: "Why don't you do something, God?!"

But remember how God answered Habakkuk in very specific terms: "I am going to do something in your days that you would not believe, even if you were told" (1:5). You know things are critical when God says that not even a prophet can imagine what He's about to do!

God's news that He was about to send the ruthless, bloodthirsty and (gulp!) Gentile Babylonians to judge His people rocked Habakkuk's world. But remember, in the face of such news, he prayed that most amazing prayer of acceptance and faith: "LORD, I have heard of your fame [could we say "glory"?]; I stand in awe of your deeds, O LORD. Renew them in our day, in our time make them known; in wrath remember mercy [grace]" (3:2). Basically, the prophet was praying, "Lord, don't lose sight of your purpose! Don't fail to uphold your character!"

Did God answer Habakkuk's prayer?

Yes!

We hear God's note of hope, even in the face of discipline, through several Old Testament prophets: Through Jeremiah God promised that the exile would last only seventy years (25:8–14). Also through Jeremiah God called the king of Babylon "my servant Nebuchadnezzar" (25:9). The prophet proclaimed, "This is what the LORD says: 'When seventy years are completed for Babylon, I will come to you and fulfill my gracious promise to bring you back to this place. For I know the plans I have for you,' declares the LORD, 'plans to prosper you and not to harm you, plans to give you hope and a future" (29:10–11). And he added, "'I will . . . bring you back from captivity. I will gather you from all the nations and places where I have banished you,' declares the LORD, 'and will bring you back to the place from which I carried you into exile.'" (29:14)

That sounds like hope!

Easy for us to say that from the comfortable seats in which we rest. But how did hope present itself to those living in Babylon?

> In the first year of Darius son of Xerxes (a Mede by descent), who was made ruler over the Babylonian kingdom—in the first year of his reign, I, Daniel, understood from the Scriptures, according to the word of the LORD given to Jeremiah the prophet, that the desolation of Jerusalem would last seventy years. So I turned to the Lord God and pleaded with him in prayer and petition, in fasting, and in sackcloth and ashes. I prayed to the LORD my God and confessed: "O Lord, the great and awesome God, who keeps his covenant of love with all who love him and obey his commands . . ." (Dan. 9:1–4)

Thus Daniel prayed, the Scriptures open before him and his heart bowed in submission to God's sovereign purposes. Then he reported this:

> While I was speaking and praying, confessing my sin and the sin of my people Israel and making my request to the LORD my God for his holy hill—while I was still in prayer, Gabriel, the man I had seen in the earlier vision, came to me in swift flight about the time of the evening sacrifice. He instructed me and said to me, "Daniel, I have now come to give you insight and understanding. As soon as you began to pray, an answer was given, which I have come to tell you, for you are highly esteemed. Therefore, consider the message and understand the vision." (9:20–23)

Young Daniel had been swept along in the first wave of exiles lifted from Jerusalem and washed up on the sands of Babylon. By now he is an old man. All these years later, he could affirm that God had never lost track of His purpose.

Daniel teaches us to open our Bible and cling to God's purpose in prayer. You may always rest in this: *God will never give up His purpose!* In fact, in a world where nothing is assured, God's purpose is the only thing that is guaranteed!

As dismayed as Habakkuk, Jeremiah and others were to hear God call Nebuchadnezzar "my servant," well before this God, through Isaiah, had said something similar about another foreign ruler, Cyrus king of the Persians:

> "He is *my shepherd* and will accomplish all that I please; he will say of Jerusalem, 'Let it be rebuilt,' and of the temple, 'Let its foundations be laid.'" This is what the LORD says to *his anointed*, to Cyrus, whose right hand I take hold of to subdue nations before him and to strip kings of their armor, to open doors before him so that gates will not be shut. (44:28–45:1)

Can you see just how incredible this is? God was going to use Nebuchadnezzar as His servant to *discipline* the people—but He was going to employ Cyrus as His servant to *restore* the people! But God is not done. He continues on, speaking of Cyrus and asserting this:

> For the sake of Jacob my servant, of Israel my chosen, I summon you by name and bestow on you a title of honor, though you do not acknowledge me. I am the LORD, and there is no other; apart from me there is no God. I will strengthen you, though you have not acknowledged me, so that from the rising of the sun to the place of its setting men may know there is none besides me. I am the LORD, and there is no other. I form the light and create darkness, I bring prosperity and create disaster; I, the LORD, do all these things. . . . This is what the LORD says—the Holy One of Israel, and its Maker: Concerning things to come, do you question me about my children, or give me orders about the work of my hands? It is I who made the earth and created mankind upon it. My own hands stretched out the heavens; I marshaled their starry

hosts. I will raise up Cyrus in my righteousness: I will make all his ways straight. He will rebuild my city and set my exiles free, but not for a price or reward, says the LORD Almighty. (45:4–7, 11–13)

To a people disciplined but still loved, God is reasserting one simple message: Trust Me!

Realize too that God was speaking of Cyrus by name approximately one hundred years before he was born. God is asserting that He not only knows what has happened, but what will happen. He is in control of it all!

So what exactly happened in time and space through this one who was named a century before he existed?

In the first year of Cyrus king of Persia, in order to fulfill the word of the LORD spoken by Jeremiah, the LORD moved the heart of Cyrus king of Persia to make a proclamation throughout his realm and to put it in writing: "This is what Cyrus king of Persia says: 'The LORD, the God of heaven, has given me all the kingdoms of the earth and he has appointed me to build a temple for him at Jerusalem in Judah. Anyone of his people among you—may his God be with him, and let him go up to Jerusalem in Judah and build the temple of the LORD, the God of Israel, the God who is in Jerusalem.'" (Ezra 1:1–3)

Remember, this decree of Cyrus's to rebuild the temple in Jerusalem did not take place until well after Isaiah's day. So who was it who brought this command about? The text declared, "*The Lord moved* the heart of Cyrus." That's *grace*! And why did He do it? It was so that the people could "build the temple of the Lord." The temple was the place where God's *glory* had formerly dwelt—and Cyrus's decree actually started the preparation process for His glory to come again!

Are you reaching for your sextant? In all the confusion, we have found once again our two fixed constants! Now we are able to take a reading on our progress toward God's one purpose.

But wait, there's more! Just as He had promised, God returned a remnant of His people to the Promised Land, starting just after King Cyrus's command. The Jews went back in three waves of repatriation. Each wave of returnees had a leader through whom God was, step by step, restoring Israel so that He could accomplish His purpose.

The first wave was led by Zerubbabel in 538 BC, with approximately fifty thousand Jews leaving exile and returning to their ancestral land (Ezra 1–6). God's purpose was for them to repopulate the land, rebuild the temple and restore the worship of God in Jerusalem. During these euphoric but challenging days, the prophets Haggai and Zechariah prophesied, encouraging the leaders and the people down the path of God's will.

The second wave of returnees arrived in the Promised Land in 458 BC under the leadership of Ezra. This man was both scribe and priest. Through his faithful ministry not only were about seventeen hundred additional Jews returned to the land, but God was restoring His Word to His people through Ezra's intentional and intensive teaching (Ezra 7–10).

The third wave of exiles came back in 445 BC under the visionary leadership of Nehemiah (Neh. 1–13). God's great purpose through Nehemiah was to restore the security of Jerusalem by rebuilding the city walls.

God is eternally faithful to His purposes. Though at times the train may appear derailed, God's objective rolls on toward its glorious and gracious fulfillment. That is as true today as it was in the heady days of Ezra, Nehemiah and their friends. It is just as certain in the details of your life at this precise moment. Are you willing to believe this? You see, God is faithful—not only to His purposes, but to His people.

God Faithfully Keeps His People

Esther is a strange and wonderful book.

It is strange because, although it is Holy Scripture, God is nowhere explicitly mentioned in its pages. Why? I suggest it is because it *seemed* He was not present or active at that time. The entire drama of Esther takes place in Persia, not in the Promised Land. It *seemed* that God had abandoned His people and cast them off forever.

On the other hand, Esther is a wonderful book because, though God's name is never found in its pages, His hand is seen everywhere in its story! When God's people thought He had disowned them forever, He extended His hand to protect and keep them. Many have asserted it, but H.A. Ironside applied this principle to the book of Esther: "God is often behind the scenes, but He moves all the scenes He is behind."[1] In fact, one man's commentary on Esther is appropriately titled *God Behind the Seen.*[2]

It's wonderful news, isn't it?

But be honest. Haven't there been times when you felt as though God were absent, uninterested and uninvolved? But even now, God is present, though you may not feel or see Him. He is always with and ever faithful to keep His people! Perhaps that truth is the very reason He brought you to these pages today.

The basic storyline of Esther might be captured in these words: God is at work behind the seen scenes! This applies to your story as well.

Review the story of Esther with me. Historically, it appears to have taken place sometime during the approximately one-hundred-year period in which the waves of exiles were returning to Israel. The Jewish people are cast away as exiles in Persia (the kingdom that superseded Babylon). They look anything but the part of a chosen, favored people. Meanwhile, within the walls of the Persian palace, a royal drama is playing out. King Xerxes (also known as Ahasuerus) and his wife are at loggerheads. His authority appears questioned; their marriage totters in the balance.

To save face and his kingdom, the king banishes his wife and, at the counsel of his advisors, seeks a new queen from among his subjects. The most beautiful women of his realm are rounded up and put through a long period of preparation before each of them auditions with the king. Mordecai, an influential man among the Jewish subjects, has a cousin (Esther) whom he has raised as his own daughter. Esther was selected for this preparation period and put on a path to the royal bedchamber. In fear she hid her ethnicity from her handlers.

As the drama plays out, Esther finds favor in the eyes of the king and is chosen to sit at his side as the new queen.

But another drama line is developing parallel to this amazing account. One of the king's closest advisors, Haman, has taken every opportunity to climb the ladder and immerse himself ever deeper into the favor of the royal court. The dramatic tension is found in the fact that Haman is an avowed anti-Semite. Further, Haman hated Mordecai because Mordecai refused to bow to him as he passed. This enraged Haman, and he plotted to have all the Jews within the Persian Empire executed.

Mordecai finds the ear of Esther and calls upon her to do what she can to deliver her people. In the face of her fears and objections, he challenges her, "Who knows but that you have come to royal position for such a time as this?" Indeed, he reminds her, "If you remain silent at this time, relief and deliverance for the Jews will arise from another place" (4:14).

Mordecai was a man of faith. He warned Esther—and through the book that bears her name, we are reminded as well—to never lose track of this great truth: God faithfully keeps His people!

Meanwhile, Haman's bitter gall moves him to prepare a gallows for Mordecai. Providentially, God gives the king a good case of insomnia. In his struggle for sleep, he calls a servant to read to him from the records of the kingdom. There, a tale of great valor is uncovered—a story about none other than Mordecai. But as

God would have it, Haman enters the royal court at the precise moment the king is querying what should be done to honor the one the king delights in. Narcissistic Haman wonders who the king could possibly delight in more than him, so he suggests a course of action—fully expecting to have these honors showered upon himself. The plan meets with the king's favor, and in a masterful turn of irony, he instructs Haman to find Mordecai and lead the charge in bestowing these honors upon him!

While Haman has been scheming, Esther has considered her cousin Mordecai's challenge and, taking her life into her hands, enters the king's presence uninvited. Grace is extended, and she invites the king and Haman to a series of banquets. As the banquets unfold, the king repeatedly inquires as to her wishes, but Esther keeps delaying the revelation of Haman's plan. Eventually, when Haman's plot to destroy her people is made known, the king turns his ire upon that man, and Haman is put to death upon the very gallows he had prepared for Mordecai!

This is one of the great dramas of all ancient literature. It is a work of art, masterfully sculpted! But the story is more than ingenious art; it is a page out of sacred history. Yet it is much more than that. The book of Esther carries a heaven-sent message to God's people through all time: God faithfully keeps His people!

This truth from Esther's story is proven true again and again to God's people over the centuries. We can distinctly see this when we take a quick look at how Israel fared under the domination of several pagan rulers.

From Nebuchadnezzar's day (about a century before Esther's) until well after the curtain rise of the next great act in God's drama, there are four great Gentile kingdoms. There was the Babylonian kingdom, under which the Jews were first led into exile and in which Daniel and his three friends stood faithfully and were preserved by God's hand. There was, as we've just recounted, the Persian kingdom, in which Esther and the exiled Jews were divinely preserved. After Persia came the Greek empire, in which a man named Mattathias and other faithful Jews would be preserved from a maniac tyrant named Antiochus IV. And finally there came the Roman Empire, in which, as we will read in the opening pages of the New Testament, faithful Jews like Simeon, Anna, Mary and Joseph would all be preserved by God's hand.

Not only did God prove His ability to preserve His people in the dire times of these empires, as He did in Esther's story, but God had also foretold the story of each of these kingdoms (Dan. 7). Each of them appears all-powerful, all-controlling and sovereign. Yet time and again the message was clearly sounded—no matter who may appear to be in charge, or even if no one seems to be at the helm, God is sovereignly on His throne, directing all events to His appointed end.

So rest in this: *No matter who seems to be in charge, God is sovereign!* It is a trustworthy statement deserving full acceptance: God is at work behind the scenes, and He moves all the scenes He is behind!

But let's be clear on one more point. Even though a remnant was in the process of returning to Israel, most of the Jews stayed permanently in exile. In these faraway lands they existed not as a separate nation, but as a sub-culture under the boot of Babylon and Persia, then Greece and then Rome. It's true that they were protected—but the "great nation" God had worked to establish was not yet fully restored. This may leave us temporarily bewildered in our journey from eternity to eternity, but we can nevertheless faithfully report that while God's people lived under foreign rulers, they were protected, and God's purpose was still advancing.

God Faithfully Keeps His Promises

As we've seen, God is always faithful to His purpose and His people. But why is this so? It's because God always faithfully keeps His promises.

God had promised His people a future, despite their rebellion against Him and the discipline of exile. And He kept those promises. The official record of His faithfulness in this matter is found as we look more closely at the return of the exiles in the books of Ezra and Nehemiah.

As I shared earlier, God returned a remnant of His people to the Promised Land in three waves, under three leaders, with three distinct but related purposes. As the people came back first under Zerubbabel's leadership and then under Ezra's, the city was repopulated and the temple rebuilt (Ezra 1–6)—but there was no divine glory in that temple:

> When the builders laid the foundation of the temple of the LORD, the priests in their vestments and with trumpets, and the Levites (the sons of Asaph) with cymbals, took their places to praise the LORD, as prescribed by David king of Israel. With praise and thanksgiving they sang to the LORD: "He is good; his love to Israel endures forever." And all the people gave a great shout of praise to the LORD, because the foundation of the house of the LORD was laid. But many of the older priests and Levites and family heads, who had seen the former temple, wept aloud when they saw the foundation of this temple being laid, while many others shouted for joy. No one could distinguish the sound of the shouts of joy from the sound of weeping, because the people made so much noise. And the sound was heard far away. (3:10–13)

As Ezra labored on in God's purposes, the Word of God was reestablished as the authority of God's people (Ezra 7–10). Ezra, we are told, "had devoted himself to the study and observance of the Law of the LORD, and to teaching its decrees and laws in Israel" (7:10). The obedience of the people at first lagged behind Ezra's teaching, but by the time we reach Ezra 9–10, we find a great confession by the people of their sin and painful steps being taken to bring their lives into conformity with God's Word.

Later, through Nehemiah, the walls of Jerusalem were restored (Neh. 1–13). But even then he was surrounded by a largely unfaithful people. Nehemiah was one of the great leaders of the Old Testament era, but he was also one of its most tortured souls. He faced an uphill climb all the way.

Sometimes, honestly, doesn't it seem this way in your life? Just remember, "If we are faithless, he remains faithful, for he cannot disown himself" (2 Tim. 2:13). Do not forget "the unchangeable character of his purpose" (Heb. 6:17, ESV). Whenever you are faced with persistent opposition in your service to God, commit your way to the Lord and pray as Nehemiah did toward the end of his recorded ministry: "*Remember me* for this, O my God, and do not blot out what I have so faithfully done for the house of my God and its services. . . . *Remember me* for this also, O my God, and show mercy to me according to your great love. . . . *Remember me* with favor, O my God" (Neh. 13:14, 22, 31).

Now as we continue considering God's faithfulness to keep His promises, let's pan out and look at things from a panoramic view. The historical books of the Old Testament—of which Nehemiah is the last—set forth what God *did*. The prophetic books, on the other hand, set forth what God *said*. So far as we have watched God keeping His promises, we have concerned ourselves mostly with things He has been doing. But His actions are really the fulfillment of things He has said. When God *says* something, we are to watch in faith for God to *do* something to fulfill what He has *said*. Let's step back for a moment and get a picture of what God was saying—the promises He was reiterating—throughout the historic scene we have been studying.

As we have walked through the books of biblical history and watched all that God has been doing, we need to note that throughout that history He has also been speaking—making amazing promises through the prophets of a coming Savior (Messiah). Remember the purpose: one man, one nation, one great Savior, so that grace might be extended and glory demonstrated to all creation! And all the time, as history has been unfolding, God has been promising this *one thing*.

The Old Testament prophets tell us of this coming Savior. In Isaiah 53 He is revealed as the Servant of the Lord who will suffer and thus atone for the sins of His people. Through Jeremiah He is designated the righteous Branch (Jer. 23:5; 33:15) and the Lord our Righteousness (23:6) who will establish a new covenant (31:31–34). Micah spoke of the precise location of the Messiah's birth (Mic. 5:2). Zechariah foretold the triumphant entry of the Messiah to Jerusalem (Zech. 9:9), His arrest and the scattering of His followers (13:7), as well as the piercing of His side (12:10).

These echoes of hope and purpose reverberate throughout the pages of the prophets. But notice now the emphasis of the final prophecies God uttered before an extended period of silence envelopes the stage.

Malachi was the last of the Old Testament prophets. He preached just after Nehemiah's time, so his words are *God's last words* of the Old Testament. God's central message through Malachi was this: "I the LORD do not change" (3:6). Basically, He was telling His people, "Although things are about to get quiet, don't fret!"

We know that at the spiritual pinnacle of Act I, God's glorious presence had descended upon His temple. This singular event had transformed Israel from a nation into a great nation. But God's shining appearance had later departed from that temple because of the enduring hardness of His people. This signaled Israel's great demise.

To this point in the scriptural record, we have no record of God's glory returning. But now, through His prophet Malachi, God says that the He will come again to His temple! True to His purpose, people and promise, God called out, "See, I will send my messenger, who will prepare the way before me. Then

suddenly the Lord you are seeking will come to his temple; the
messenger of the covenant, whom you desire, will come" (3:1).

God was promising that He would come again, gloriously,
to the temple He had previously abandoned. And before His return, a forerunner—a messenger—would be sent to prepare His
way. Indeed, as the book of Malachi closes (and with it the entire
Old Testament), God uses His final pen strokes to declare, "See,
I will send you the prophet Elijah before that great and dreadful
day of the LORD comes" (4:5).

That may not all make perfect sense now, but soon enough
the dots will begin to connect. Just remember what God has said
here. You'll discover that the last words from God's lips in the
Old Testament will be, after four hundred years of silence, the
first words from His lips in the New Testament.

For now, just rest in this: *God's last word is His first priority!*

Before we conclude this scene, let's ask ourselves once more:
Where are we with the divine drama line, God's purpose statement? His plan is to use one man (Abraham) to build one great
nation (Israel) through whom He will provide the one Savior
(Jesus) who will reveal God's glory and extend God's grace to all
creation.

Thus far we have seen God take one man and make him
into a great nation. Unfortunately, that nation fell, but by God's
grace the people are now restored and magnificent promises of
an infinite grace have been made.

Now we wait. The curtain has dropped. Looming before us
is an interlude of four hundred silent years!

Writing Your Story

During the quiet times—the times when it seems God is not
present, that He does not hear and is not active—never forget:
God faithfully keeps His purposes, His people and His promises. Just before the curtain dropped on the final scene of this

act, God exhorted us to recall, even in the silence, "I the LORD do not change" (Mal. 3:6).

Think for a moment about all those times you've been in mid-sentence on the cell phone and suddenly the call is dropped. You wait for a response from the other party, but you are met with only silence. It makes you a little nervous, doesn't it? You wonder, was the call just dropped? Or did they hang up on me?

Know this in the quiet times, in the dark times, in the times when God seems disinterested and distant: God does not change. He never gives up His purpose. No matter who seems to be in charge, God is sovereign. God's last word is His first priority.

Reviewing God's Story

God is faithful to His _____,

His _____ and His _____.

So we can rest in this:

1. God will never give up His _____.

2. No matter who seems to be in charge, God is in

    _____.

3. God's last word is His first _____.

Remembering God's Story

Scriptures	Ezra–Esther, Haggai–Malachi
Key Characters	Cyrus, Zerubbabel, Ezra, Esther, Nehemiah, Haggai, Zechariah, Malachi
Key Events	Cyrus returns the Jews to their land, three groups return to Jerusalem, Jews preserved in Persia, rebuilding of the temple, rebuilding of Jerusalem's walls
Key Verse	"This is what the Lord says: 'When seventy years are completed for Babylon, I will come to you and fulfill my gracious promise to bring you back to this place.'" Jeremiah 29:10

God's Story

Eternity Past

← Creation
← Fall / Flood / Babel   } Gen. 1–11

2,000 yrs. {
← The Rise of Israel
← Temple ⚡ **GLORY!**   } Gen. 12–1 Kings 10

400 yrs. {
← The Decline of Israel
← Exile! → **GLORY!**   } 1 Kings 11–2 Chron., Prov.

140 yrs. {
← Exiles Return after 70 years
← Temple Rebuilt
← Walls Restored   } Ezra–Esther, Hag.–Mal.

Eternity Future

Interlude

A Silent Grace
Between the Testaments

The curtain has dropped. The applause has died away. The stage is empty. The story that has been unfolding now simply hangs unresolved in the air. As the theater becomes shrouded in silence, people shift in their seats. Furtive glances are cast between bewildered faces. As one, although without speaking, everyone wonders: *What has become of the story? Why is nothing happening? Why this silence?!*

Silence is scary. A great many find the absence of sound a menacing, intimidating thing. This alone may explain the constant "noise" of our society. TV, iPod, radio, computer, cell phone—nearly any device will suffice if it fills up the terrifying holes in the noise of life. We are ill at ease with silence. The voids in the fabric of sound seem to expose the nakedness of our souls.

James Freedman, president of Dartmouth College, observed, "Everywhere we look, the world urges us to turn on the radio or TV, to make a phone call, to see a movie. Many of us, I fear, worry that, if left alone with our thoughts and feelings, we may discover that we do not make very good company for ourselves."[1] Henri Nouwen agrees: "In this chatty society, silence has become a fearful thing. For most people, silence creates itchiness and nervousness. Many experience silence not as full and rich, but as empty and hollow. For them silence is like a gapping abyss which can swallow them up."[2]

The Significance of Silence

Part of the problem, I suppose, is that silence must be interpreted. And silence can be interpreted in a variety of ways.

Some read silence as *isolation.* The absence of sound speaks to them of rejection and abandonment.

Others feel that silence indicates *intensity.* That is to say that silence adds dramatic effect—it increases tension and heightens expectation. It's the part in the movie or play when the background music and sound effects evaporate while the main character creeps through the house seeking the source of some eerie sound.

Silence can even signify *intimacy.* Is there someone in your life whose presence you enjoy even in long periods of silence? The closeness this produces is precisely what enables many couples, after a lifetime of marriage, to know the thoughts or the next words of one another—they have no need for words, for the eyes say it all. Their silence broadcasts a deep intimacy forged over many years and innumerable conversations.

I remind you that when the New Testament will eventually open with Matthew 1:1, heaven will have been silent for four hundred years. Most today would not be surprised by such quietude—they would think it strange if heaven should speak at all. But we need to remember that these four hundred years of silence follow four to five hundred years of incessant divine weeping and pleading, as voiced by the prophets. And this silence comes on the heels of scores of prophetic promises which heralded the next stage in God's eternal plan—the sending of one great Savior!

The fact is, this divine silence made the people uneasy. As J. Sidlow Baxter has observed, the words of Psalm 74:9 may represent the experience of Israel during those soundless centuries:

"We are given no miraculous signs; no prophets are left, and none of us knows how long this will be."[3]

Silence Is Not Inactivity

Silence, however, does not necessarily indicate inactivity. *The fact that God has not been speaking does not mean that God has not been moving.* Is that the very word you need to hear at this moment? Take a moment and reread that sentence. In fact, stop and meditate upon it. Underline it. Come back to it again. *The fact that God has not been speaking does not mean that God has not been moving.*

St. John of the Cross described what he called the "night of the senses," a season of time when it seems impossible to enjoy the presence of God and to sense His nearness. Through such a vacuous season of life, the only option is to live and move by faith alone, since all emotion and all sense of God's presence and grace seem to have been suspended. Has God providentially landed you in just such a season?

Or perhaps you are in the midst of a deeper type of darkness that St. John called the "dark night of the soul"—a season of time in which God seems to have entirely abandoned you and a dreadful sense of condemnation for your sins looms large over your soul.[4] It is not that God has abandoned you. No, His promises still stand. But in the silence of that "dark night of the soul," it *feels* as if He has.

Silence is tricky stuff. "Silence," says A.A. Attanasio, "is a text easy to misread."[5] It does seem that way.

Perhaps that is what we can learn best from John Cage, an avant-garde American composer. Cage composed a piece of "music" known as 4'33"—a composition in which no notes are played. None. Zip. Zero. Zilch. Nada. Mr. Cage insists that there are in fact three movements to the piece. But the music consists of nothing but silence—four minutes and thirty-three seconds filled with it. The listener is simply invited to hear the silence—or perhaps what the silence reveals.

Researchers tell us that brief periods of sensory deprivation can be relaxing. Indeed, many seek out such solitude. Quakers purposefully build a period of silence into their corporate worship experiences. But over extended periods of time, sensory deprivation tends to produce anxiety, apprehension, hallucinations, bizarre thought patterns, unsociable behavior and despair. Studies show that the vast majority of people left in a soundproof room for more than a few minutes reported hearing tinnitus-like sounds.[6] In layman's terms—they began hearing things that simply were not there.

What is true in individual experience can also find parallels in corporate experience. Thus, we do well to get our bearings during this interlude in God's unfolding story. So before the curtain opens on Act II, we need to ask, What goes on in the dark four hundred years of silence, after the prophet Malachi speaks the final words of the Old Testament prophetic era?

Remember, God has been working out one divine, eternal plan throughout all of history: choosing one man (Abraham) and making of him one great nation (Israel) so that through them He might bring one great Savior (Jesus Christ) that He might extend His grace and demonstrate His glory to all creation. So what is God doing in all this silence? Working that plan to the next great stage! This is what God is *always* up to in the silences of life.

Later in the New Testament we will be told, "But when the time had fully come, God sent his Son, born of a woman, born under law" (Gal. 4:4). Just exactly how was God preparing the world for the exact moment of Jesus' incarnation so that the Messiah's coming might be truly in "the fullness of time" (NASB)? A number of key world developments are often pointed to as being a part of those divine preparations.

One such development was *the spread of the Greek language*. By the time of Christ, the Greek language was used throughout the known world, and its familiarity was preparing the way for the rapid spread of the Good News. During these years of silence, God also moved in the hearts of men to translate the Hebrew Scriptures into Greek. That translation became known as the Septuagint, from the Latin word *septuaginta*, meaning seventy (and thus abbreviated with LXX). (It is so called because tradition tells us that the translation was the work of seventy Jewish elders during the reign of the Greek kingdom, somewhere between 284–247 BC.)[7] The Septuagint became the most widely used version of the Scriptures in the time before Jesus appeared on the scene. After Jesus came and then died, rose and ascended to heaven, the apostles were able to take the gospel to a world which had become familiar with the words of God through this Greek translation of the Hebrew Scriptures.

The rise of Jewish synagogues was another evidence of divine preparation. Most of the Jews who had been taken into exile did not return to the land of Israel. Rather, they took seriously the divine command they had been given to "seek the peace and prosperity of the city to which I have carried you into exile. Pray to the LORD for it, because if it prospers, you too will prosper" (Jer. 29:7). Although they settled in to their new localities, they did not want to spiritually assimilate to the culture around them. Thus, they began to rally themselves around God's Word, which they had brought with them from the Promised Land. Buildings known as synagogues became their gathering places. So by the New Testament era, synagogues were scattered over the surface of the then-known world. These synagogues became points of contact for advancing missionaries as they sought to spread the news of Jesus, the promised Messiah. Wherever these preachers of the gospel went, they looked for synagogues as a first point of contact because they knew that there the Scriptures would have already plowed the ground of people's hearts and prepared them to receive the seed of the Good News.

Another development that made for "the fullness of time"

was *the Roman Peace* (*Pax Romana*). The world was under the dominance of Rome and thus was relatively free of warfare—making for good conditions and enabling missionaries of the gospel to move easily throughout the kingdom. The early church did not have an easy assignment, but as they spread out across the earth, they did so in times which were relatively free from the dangers and devastations of warfare.

Additionally, *the Roman road system* made travel easier than it had ever been. This would become essential as the apostles were sent out with the gospel of Jesus Christ to the far corners of the earth. God was preparing the worldwide delivery systems along which the news of His one great Savior would travel!

Clearly, just because God had not been speaking does not mean that He had not been moving. He had, even though in silence. This is good news for *all* of us—for God was working to provide the world a Savior. This is good news for *each* of us—for in our personal experience we sometimes feel abandoned when things fall silent for a time.

Silence Is Not Retroactive

There is yet another principle to be discovered in the silence. Like the first, it too gives us great hope and direction: *Just because God has been silent does not mean He has not spoken.* Have you ever considered that the reason God may not be speaking now is because He has already spoken? And if He has, then why should we expect Him to repeat Himself? If God is not speaking at present, it may be that He has already told us what He is doing at present and that He's even told us how to understand what is transpiring around us.

This was true in the four hundred silent years between the Testaments. Before God fell silent, He spoke. He did so through the prophet Daniel, unfolding to him what was about to transpire during these years of silence.

God used several dreams to reveal to His people what the

coming generations would face as He prepared to send His Son as the one great Savior of the world. The first dream came to the unbelieving king of Babylon, Nebuchadnezzar, and was interpreted by Daniel. The dream revolved around a great statue:

> The head of the statue was made of pure gold, its chest and arms of silver, its belly and thighs of bronze, its legs of iron, its feet partly of iron and partly of baked clay. While you were watching, a rock was cut out, but not by human hands. It struck the statue on its feet of iron and clay and smashed them. Then the iron, the clay, the bronze, the silver and the gold were broken to pieces at the same time and became like chaff on a threshing floor in the summer. The wind swept them away without leaving a trace. But the rock that struck the statue became a huge mountain and filled the whole earth. (Dan. 2:32–35)

As God unfolded the meaning of this dream to Daniel, He made clear that He was foretelling the existence of the four great empires which would rule the world leading up to the time of the Messiah's advent. The first, as you will remember, was Nebuchadnezzar's own Babylonian empire (2:38). This kingdom would give way to the Medo-Persian empire, which in turn would give way to the Greek empire (2:39). Finally, the Roman empire would be established and in place when God's Savior was revealed to the world (2:40).

In a later dream, this time to Daniel himself, God underscored this revelation of the four empires who would rule during the time that heavenly silence would envelop the earth (Dan. 7). This dream was of terrifying beasts, each one representing one of the kingdoms: a lion with wings like an eagle (Babylon, 7:4), a bear (Medo-Persia, 7:5), a leopard (Greece, 7:6) and a "terrifying and frightening and very powerful" beast (Rome, 7:7). This last beast "had large iron teeth; it crushed and devoured its victims and trampled underfoot whatever was left. It was different from all the former beasts, and it had ten horns" (7:7).

God went on to describe, in Daniel 8, the Medo-Persian and Greek kingdoms. From there He went even further, describing in chapter 11 some of these kingdoms in amazing detail. Of this chapter Donald Campbell asserts that "in the first 35 verses there are at least 135 prophecies that have been literally fulfilled and can be corroborated by a study of the history of the period."[8]

Why is this significant? Because it tells us that God knew the history of the silent years *before it took place*! It reminds us that just because God is not speaking, it does not mean He has not spoken!

In fact, in addition to explaining events that would happen during the silent years, God even spoke directly of the coming days of silence. He repeatedly warned Israel about them: "'The days are coming,' declares the Sovereign LORD, 'when I will send a famine through the land—not a famine of food or a thirst for water, but a famine of hearing the words of the LORD'" (Amos 8:11). "Calamity upon calamity will come, and rumor upon rumor. They will try to get a vision from the prophet; the teaching of the law by the priest will be lost, as will the counsel of the elders" (Ezek. 7:26). "Therefore night will come over you, without visions, and darkness, without divination. The sun will set for the prophets, and the day will go dark for them. The seers will be ashamed and the diviners disgraced. They will all cover their faces because there is no answer from God" (Mic. 3:6–7).

But God assured Israel that the silence would not last forever: "Although the Lord gives you the bread of adversity and the water of affliction, your teachers will be hidden no more; with your own eyes you will see them. Whether you turn to the right or to the left, your ears will hear a voice behind you, saying, 'This is the way; walk in it'" (Isa. 30:20–21).

This is instructive for us now, for you may feel that God has fallen silent in your life. But this does not mean He has not spoken, nor that He is not now speaking through the revealed

Scriptures by His Holy Spirit. Indeed, in one sense, heaven has gone silent again—in terms of giving inspired Scripture. But it does not mean He has not spoken. No, He has already explained to us what He is up to now and told us how we should view what is transpiring around us. This is the very purpose of the Scripture and one of the Holy Spirit's primary ministries in this age.

Learning to Listen in the Silence

What was happening redemptively with Israel can happen to us individually. That is to say, these two great principles we have just contemplated are true not only on the macro-scale but on the micro-scale, not only collectively but personally. There is—despite what you may feel at the moment—a redemptive element to heaven's silences. One could even say that silence is the gymnasium where our souls exercise themselves and grow strong in faith. The people of God who have been willing to wait upon Him in the silence have always found it so.

Job endured epic pain and apparent abandonment without so much as a word from heaven about the cosmic wager for his soul. Abraham logged many miles and many years between the giving of God's promises and their affirmations, let alone their fulfillment. Joseph, whose troubles started because of heaven-sent dreams, found himself in Egypt interpreting the dreams of others, though now apparently bereft of his own. Samuel pressed through, even though "in those days the word of the LORD was rare; there were not many visions" (1 Sam. 3:1). The apostles of Christ were left for ten days without word from heaven, but were simply told to "stay in the city until [they had] been clothed with power from on high" (Luke 24:49).

How then do we come into possession of the kinds of advantages these saints eventually gained? How do we wring hope from the rag of apparent ruin? Consider David. In the seemingly vacuous years between his initial anointing and his actual arrival at Israel's throne, he must surely have wondered at the silences of God. Yet it is David who teaches us so much about redeeming the silent spans of life.

David began Psalm 62 by declaring, "My soul waits in silence for God only" (62:1, NASB). It might be rendered more literally, "Only to God [in] silence [is] my soul." The key word of this verse is translated from the Hebrew as "waits in silence," but it is difficult to find an appropriate English rendering, one that will convey all its meaning. It has the notion of both to wait and to repose. The Lutheran scholar Leupold insists that it is ultimately untranslatable.[9] Allan Harman asserts that it is Godward in its focus and describes "a quiet waiting for salvation which comes exclusively from him."[10] This Hebrew word describes not just waiting in silence, but waiting in silence on God. No other knock is answered; no other call is taken. No outside help is looked to or welcomed. No alternative options are left open and no contingencies entertained.

Additionally, in this psalm the Hebrew word translated "only" is found six times (62:1, 2, 4, 5, 6, 9). It peppers the prayer with an absolute, exclusive taste. I hear many people talk about trusting God, but I hear relatively few assert their trust in God only. For most, God is added to their list of options—kept near at hand in the event He is needed. His number is placed in the speed dial, "just in case."

But God will have none of this; nor will the soul that has known His silences—and yet still longs for Him who is the Word.

The steel of one's soul is tempered in the silences of life until it comes to the kind of repose we see here in David. Such rest is not arrived at without some work. Even the psalmist admits this, for despite his faith-filled assertion at the opening of the psalm, it is not long before he is counseling himself: "My soul, wait in silence for God only, for my hope is from Him" (62:5, NASB). Again, this may more literally be rendered, "Only to God be silent my soul."

Perhaps the key is found in verse 8: "Trust in him at all times, O people; pour out your hearts to him, for God is our refuge." This "at all times" kind of trust includes seasons of silence as well as times of hearing God speak. The invitation-imperative to "pour out your hearts" to God means that while things may seem silent from the top down, things must never be silent from the bottom up. When you "pour out" the contents of your heart, you utterly empty it of all that has been brewing in the silence— the fear, anxiety, obsessive thoughts, dread and worry. These silent thieves of our inner joy must become articulated if they are to be defeated. In this way we discover that "God is our refuge." This is precisely how we "trust in him at all times."

Silence Is an Invitation

I am reminded that in music, silence is not simply silence. Musically, a silence is called a rest. David was a musician. It seems to me—though I am no musician—that the key to understanding the silence in music is never to lose sight of the notes immediately before and after it. Connecting the dots between those notes and interpreting the silence in its context transforms silence into rest. Context, musically speaking, instructs us as to how to read the silence.

The same is true spiritually. Trouble is, when you're in the midst of silence, you haven't yet heard the next note. All you have are the notes that have gone before. The music that led you to this moment only tells you that something is now unresolved. It leaves you listening, longing for those notes which will resolve the melody that has been played out to this point. Here— between the Testaments—we have heard enough to know that God's story is not resolved. We need to trust the Conductor enough to know that He has more notes yet to be played. Only in this kind of faith-rest can we be ready to hear the next notes in this strain of divine music.

Indeed, psychologists tell us of the positive effects of silence on both concentration and learning. You know what that is like—a speaker is not audible to you, so you lean in, focus your eyes upon the person's lips, cup your hands to your ears and strive to block out any interference. Why not take the apparent silence in your life as an invitation to do that right now in your relationship with God?

You may just discover that "silence is the element in which great things fashion themselves together; that at length they may emerge, full-formed and majestic, into the daylight of Life, which they are thenceforth to rule."[11] It will prove true in God's grand story as in due time the curtain rises again on the stage of human history and the eternal purposes of God continue to unfold before us. May it prove true also in your personal story as you wait upon Him who is behind all the scenes—and who moves all the scenes He is behind.

Writing Your Story

Sir Robert Anderson was correct when he said, "A silent heaven is the greatest mystery of our existence."[12] As you wait upon God and perhaps wonder at what seems an interminable silence from heaven, remember the following truths:

- Whatever God is doing in the silence, it is *redemptive*. Redemption is not just something God *does,* but something He *is*—Redeemer is His very name (Job 19:25; Ps. 19:14). God aims to prove the greatness of His glory as a giver.

- Whatever God is doing in the silence, it is *purposeful.* God never moves without intention. He wastes nothing. He moves steadily toward the fulfillment of His one great plan. This is true even in periods of silence.

- Whatever God is doing in the silence, it is *good, loving, gracious* and *kind.* As Charles Spurgeon has often been quoted as saying, "God is too good to be unkind, too wise to be mistaken, and when you cannot trace His hand, you can always trust His heart."

- Whatever God is doing in the silence, it is about His *glory*. Remember, everything about everything is about the glory of God.

- Whatever God is doing in the silence, it is *not without warning*: "Surely the Sovereign LORD does nothing without revealing his plan to his servants the prophets" (Amos 3:7). Just because it may seem God is not speaking, it does not mean He has not spoken. Cry out to God for illumination and expect that He will grant it as you pore over what God has said in His Word (Ps. 119:130).

Reviewing God's Story

Before you close these pages, take a few moments to review what we have discovered in the darkness and silence of this interlude in God's story.

1. Silence does not equal inactivity: The fact that God has not been _____ does not mean that He has not been _____.

2. Silence is not retroactive: Just because God has been _____ does not mean He has not _____.

3. Silence is an invitation: "My soul waits in _____ for God _____" (Ps. 62:1, NASB).

Remembering God's Story

Scriptures	Between the Old and New Testaments

Key Characters	Alexander the Great; Antiochus IV (Epiphanes), Mattathias, the Sanhedrin, Scribes, Essenes, Pharisees, Saducees and Herodians

Key Events	Medo-Persian, Greek and Roman Empires; division of the Greek empire; Maccabean revolt; translation of Septuagiant; spread of Greek language; Roman road system; *Pax Romana*; rise of Jewish synagogues

Key Verse	"We are given no miraculous signs; no prophets are left, and none of us knows how long this will be." Psalm 74:9

Eternity Past

← Creation

← Fall / Flood / Babel

← The Rise of Israel

← Temple GLORY!

← The Decline of Israel

← Exile! → GLORY!

← Restoration of a Remnant

← 400 Years of SILENCE!

Eternity Future

2,000 yrs.

400 yrs.

140 yrs.

400 yrs.

Gen. 1–11

Gen. 12–
1 Kings 10

1 Kings 11
–2 Chron.,
Prov.

Ezra–
Esther,
Hag.–Mal.

God's Story

ACT II, SCENE 1

A Saving Grace
Matthew–John

It's been well over a year now; four hundred sixty-eight days to be exact. I sent an important request via letter over fifteen months ago, and I am still awaiting a response. I've followed it up with several e-mails, requesting a reply. But I've heard nothing. Total silence. I sent another letter, and then yet another. Still there has been no response.

How does one interpret such silence? What inference should be drawn? Actually, interpreting silence is easy—it is interpreting it *accurately* that is difficult. So I must ask, what am I to make of this deafening silence?

This must have been something like how the Jews felt after not four hundred days but four hundred years of waiting for God's next word. It is difficult to find rest in the music until the notes following it are played. But now, finally, after a long, awkward interlude of silence, the curtain is about to open on Act II, Scene 1. Thus, the stage has been set for a whole new act in God's eternal plan.

I forewarned you that the last word God spoke in the Old Testament would be the first one He would speak as the New Testament opened. The last word from the prophets (and of the entire Old Testament) was this:

See, I will send you the prophet Elijah before that great and dreadful day of the LORD comes. He will turn the hearts of the fathers to their children, and the hearts of the children to their fathers; or else I will come and strike the land with a curse. (Mal. 4:5–6)

Chronologically, the next words God spoke came via an angel, who picked up exactly where God had left off four hundred years earlier. The angel announced the words to Zechariah, who was about to become the father of John the Baptist, and he told Zechariah of his son's purpose—that he was to be the very "Elijah" spoken of by the prophet Malachi.

And he will go on before the Lord, in the spirit and power of Elijah, to turn the hearts of the fathers to their children and the disobedient to the wisdom of the righteous—to make ready a people prepared for the Lord. (Luke 1:17)

John the Baptist was the divinely appointed herald to prepare the way before Jesus. His birth was signaling a remarkable leap forward in the fulfillment of God's plan to use one man (Abraham) to build one great nation (Israel) through whom He would provide the one Savior (Jesus) who would reveal God's glory and extend God's grace to all people. The Savior expected for thousands of years was about to step upon the stage of human history! The One who would usher God's plan into fulfillment would soon take His place before us! God's silence was about to be broken in remarkable fashion.

But why, we might ask, was Jesus the perfect way for God to break the silence? Consider the Bible's answer in the following seven realities.

In Jesus, God Was Speaking to Us

John's Gospel opens very much like Genesis does: "In the beginning was the Word, and the Word was with God, and the

Word was God" (1:1). But this New Testament Word, unlike the one in Genesis, was made tangible (1:14) so that the very physical presence of Christ would be a statement made by God. "In the past God spoke to our forefathers through the prophets at many times and in various ways, but in these last days he has spoken to us by his Son, whom he appointed heir of all things, and through whom he made the universe" (Heb. 1:1–2).

John's choice of "Word" (*logos*) to describe Jesus had profound implications. This word "logos" was used in Greek philosophy to describe the reason or order which stands behind the universe. The fact that there are consistent, repeated, reliable laws of nature was, in the Gentile mind, evidence of a "word" standing behind what we can see and touch. This "word" is what keeps the world beyond the grasp of chaos. The Gentile reader of John's day would read that Jesus is "the Word" and understand that to mean that He is the one who orders the universe, holding it all together in a reliable, consistent way. Indeed, the Bible says Jesus is "sustaining all things by his powerful word" (Heb. 1:3) and that "in him all things hold together" (Col. 1:17).

The Jewish readers of John's Gospel, however, would likely not have understood his use of logos in the same way. Their minds would have raced back to a string of Old Testament Scriptures which speak of the *power* of God's word: "God said, 'Let there be . . .'" is the repeated refrain of Genesis 1. And each time He spoke, the divine Word produced things like light, expanse, dry ground, green things, living things! From the very beginning the Word never shot a blank. Whatever He said was done! "By the word of the LORD were the heavens made, their starry host by the breath of his mouth" (Ps. 33:6). "He sent forth His word and healed them" (107:20). "So will my word be which goes forth from My mouth; it will not return to Me empty, without accomplishing what I desire, and without succeeding in the matter for which I sent it" (Isa. 55:11, NASB).

Clearly, Jesus was not just another individual to walk the

earth; He was utterly unique—and in Him God was speaking
to you and to me. This baby was God in flesh! He was "'Im-
manuel'—which means, 'God with us'" (Matt. 1:23; see also Isa.
7:14). Luke writes of the shepherds that "the *glory* of the Lord
shone about them," and the angels sang, "*Glory* to God in the
highest" (Luke 2:9, 14). Joseph was instructed to name the baby
"Jesus, because he will *save* [that's grace!] his people from their
sins" (Matt. 1:21). From the moment of Jesus' conception and
through all the circumstances of His birth, God was speaking
glory and grace! But God had a great deal more to say through
Jesus.

In Jesus, God Was Dwelling among Us

John reports, "The Word became flesh and made his dwelling among us. We have seen his *glory*, the *glory* of the One and
Only, who came from the Father, full of *grace* and truth" (John
1:14).

Do you see it? Jesus unveils the glory and grace of God in
our midst. The expression "made his dwelling" might more literally be rendered "tabernacled." The tabernacle was the precursor
to the temple and, like the temple, was the place where God
made His glory dwell. Jesus' body became the new temple. Thus,
He could say, "I tell you that one greater than the temple is here"
(Matt. 12:6). On one occasion Jesus said, "Destroy this temple,
and I will raise it again in three days." Then those arguing with
Him replied, "It has taken forty-six years to build this temple,
and you are going to raise it in three days?" John answered that
question by adding, "But the temple he had spoken of was his
body" (John 2:19–21).

God had shown His glory to Abraham when He called Him.
He had made Israel a great nation when He came in glory to
inhabit the temple built by Solomon. He had disciplined the nation when He withdrew His glory from that temple in the days
of Ezekiel. But now, in the Person of Jesus, God was stepping

back into time and space and moving toward His people again.

God "pitched His tent" among us as a Man so that we could *hear* what was previously *inaudible* ("The Word became flesh," 1:14), *see* what was previously *invisible* ("We have seen his glory, the glory of the One and Only," 1:14), *understand* what was previously *inexplicable* ("No one has ever seen God, but God the One and Only, who is at the Father's side, has made him known," 1:18) and *experience* what was previously *impossible* ("From the fullness of his grace we have all received one blessing after another. For the law was given through Moses; grace and truth came through Jesus Christ," 1:16–17)!

In Jesus, God Was Working among Us

Jesus performed many miracles. He turned water to wine, calmed angry seas, walked on water and multiplied loaves and fishes to feed thousands. He healed the lepers, the blind and the paralyzed. Jesus delivered people from demonic oppression, and He raised the dead. Peter summarized it all this way: "God anointed Jesus of Nazareth with the Holy Spirit and power, and . . . he went around doing good and healing all who were under the power of the devil, because God was with him" (Acts 10:38).

Jesus did this for two great reasons: to show compassion (see Matt. 14:14) and to make a statement—or in other words, to show "signs" (John 20:30). A sign communicates a message via words or symbols. A sign says something. So God, through Jesus' miraculous actions and works, was speaking to us.

What was God saying through His Son? Simply this: In Jesus I am invading your space! Jesus was unambiguous: "If I drive out demons by the Spirit of God, then the kingdom of God has come upon you" (Matt. 12:28). To Pharisees hostile to Him, Jesus warned, "Behold, the kingdom of God is in your midst" (Luke 17:21). That is to say, the King had come and was in their midst, and by rejecting Him they were in danger of rejecting the very kingdom they claimed to serve!

In Jesus, God Was Obeying for Us

As Jesus lived His life, what was He doing? By this I mean more than just the miracles and teaching, but all of it—all the eating, drinking, walking and building relationships. Why did Jesus spend His time the way He did? Why did He build tables and chairs? And why did He build them the way He did? In short, what was He doing in all the details of life?

The Bible answers with ringing clarity. In every moment, at every place, in everything, Jesus was living the only perfect life ever lived. Jesus was living the righteous life we should have lived, but haven't. Jesus was tempted, but He never sinned. In fact, He was "tempted in every way, just as we are—yet was without sin" (Heb. 4:15). Peter could say that Jesus "committed no sin, and no deceit was found in his mouth" (1 Pet. 2:22). John emphatically stated, "In him is no sin" (1 John 3:5).

But Jesus not only turned from sin at every point of life, He embraced righteousness at every turn. He not only successfully avoided moral failure, He positively fulfilled every righteous requirement of the Father in every moment of His life. When Jesus presented Himself to John the Baptist as a candidate for baptism, John balked, believing he was no one to be baptizing the Son of God. Jesus said, however, "It is proper for us to do this *to fulfill all righteousness*" (Matt. 3:15).

That's what Jesus was doing. At every moment, in every event, with every word, every thought, every encounter and every relationship—He was fulfilling all righteousness. Jesus never sinned. But He also actively, continuously, unfailingly, positively fulfilled every righteous requirement of God the Father. Jesus, in His earthly life, in dependence upon the Holy Spirit, fulfilled every demand, command and requirement of God. And He did so perfectly.

Jesus did this not just for Himself, but for us. Thus, when He died, He was not there for sins of His own but for ours. And thus, when He rose, He was able to extend to us a clean slate as well as a ledger with our name on it, to which God recorded all the righteousness of Jesus as if it were our very own.

Indeed, God the Father declares Jesus' righteousness to be our own. The Bible calls this justification. Justification is often defined as God declaring that you are "just as if you'd never sinned." That would be a wonderful gift—but it is short-sighted. The fact is that justification is far better than even that. Justification, as Jerry Bridges has said, is God declaring that you are "*just as if you'd always obeyed.*"

Do you see the difference? The former promises your sins will not be counted against you, but it leaves you in a neutral state before God—no sin counted against you, but still devoid of the positive righteousness God requires of you (Matt. 5:48). The second offers assurance of sins forgiven, but it also offers the assurance that God has determined to ever and always view you as the possessor of Jesus' perfect life of obedience!

Jesus offers to do more than just wipe your sins away; He also causes His perfect obedience to be recorded over all the pages of your life. "God made him who had no sin to be sin for us, so that in him *we might become the righteousness of God*" (2 Cor. 5:21). As such, I am not dependent upon "a righteousness of my own that comes from the law" but upon "that which is through faith in Christ—*the righteousness that comes from God* and is by faith" (Phil 3:9).

In Jesus, God was Redeeming Us

As Jesus went about His earthly ministry, He was basically doing one thing in all His teaching, in all His healing, in all His interactions—He was presenting Himself to the world as God in the flesh, the Father's Messiah, the sovereign King, the only Savior. At every turn He was giving people the opportunity to embrace Him, to entrust themselves to Him.

Jesus' earthly ministry came to a culmination when at the

end of approximately three years He came to Jerusalem for the Passover festival. As He came, some welcomed Him as the messianic king promised by God. They shouted, "Hosanna to the Son of David!" (Matt. 21:9) and "Blessed is the king who comes in the name of the Lord!" (Luke 19:38). They waved palm branches to express their acceptance of Christ as their king. But there were others, like the Jewish rulers, who rejected Jesus as their Messiah. Some of them demanded, "Teacher, rebuke your disciples!" (Luke 19:39). But Jesus replied, "I tell you . . . , if they keep quiet, the stones will cry out" (19:40).

Having entered Jerusalem, Jesus went directly to the temple. Why did He do so? Why were the Scripture writers careful to record this event? *Because God Himself was coming back to the temple after having absented Himself in Ezekiel's day!* Do not allow yourself to miss the historical and dramatic import of this moment in God's unfolding plan. Let your mind frame this event with the scenes that have gone before in this drama. Scripture was being fulfilled!

> Lift up your heads, O you gates; be lifted up, you ancient doors, that the King of glory may come in. Who is this King of glory? The LORD strong and mighty, the LORD mighty in battle. Lift up your heads, O you gates; lift them up, you ancient doors, that the King of glory may come in. Who is he, this King of glory? The LORD Almighty—he is the King of glory. (Ps. 24:7–10)

Tragically, Jesus found that the temple had not been prepared for Him. Consequently, He drove the buyers and sellers from it and, if we have eyes to see, we will apprehend that the glory of God once again withdrew from His temple.

A few days later Jesus was arrested and sent through a mockery of trials. He was beaten, scourged and humiliated. Then He was crucified. Six hours later, hanging upon the cross, Jesus died.

This is one of the most familiar stories of human history.

But, lest we miss its importance, I ask, what was it all about?

The answer is that Jesus was there dying my death, paying my fine, standing in my place, enduring my hell. "The wages of sin is death" (Rom. 6:23). The "LORD has laid on him the iniquity of us all" (Isa. 53:6). "He himself bore our sins in his body on the tree" (1 Pet. 2:24). That day you were purchased, and God Himself wrapped His strong hands around the title deed to your life.

Do you recall where we began this new act? "But when the time had fully come, God sent his Son, born of a woman, born under law, *to redeem* those under law, that we might receive the full rights of sons" (Gal. 4:4–5). Jesus "gave himself for us to redeem us from all wickedness and to purify for himself a people that are his very own" (Titus 2:14). "You are not your own; you were bought at a price" (1 Cor. 6:19–20).

In Jesus, God Was Victorious for Us

God the Father did not abandon Jesus to death. After three days God raised Him from the dead. Jesus was "declared with power to be the Son of God by his resurrection from the dead" (Rom. 1:4). Indeed, "since Christ was raised from the dead, he cannot die again; death no longer has mastery over him" (6:9). The Bible says that the last enemy to be defeated is death—and Jesus has already secured that victory via His own resurrection from the dead. Thus, we have hope not just of forgiveness, but of life that lasts forever! Jesus lives now "in the power of an indestructible life" (Heb. 7:16).

But we have more than that. Eternal life is not just a *thing*. Eternal life is not something simply relegated to a far distant time in a vastly different realm. Eternal life begins now for the person who surrenders in faith to Christ. Jesus Himself asserted, "This is eternal life: that they may know you, the only true God, and Jesus Christ, whom you have sent" (John 17:3). Eternal life is not a thing to be obtained, but a Person to be embraced. Jesus comes to dwell within us and to be our life. Paul declared, "I no longer live, but Christ lives in me. The life I live in the body, I live by faith in the Son of God" (Gal. 2:20). Indeed, he went so far as to say, "Christ . . . is your life" (Col. 3:4)!

Eternal life is not just about quantity of time (everlasting life) but about quality of existence (overcoming life). This overcoming aspect of eternal life gives us the confidence that Jesus can do more than just forgive us when we sin. He is actually able to break the power of sin in your life *now*. He does so not by a list of rules; His liberty is not found in dos and don'ts. *He produces* this freedom *within you* by coming to live His life (the only righteous life) in and through you. And you give Him permission to do so through your faith-filled steps of obedience.

In Jesus, God Is Ruling for Us

Too often this is where people stop in recounting the life of Jesus—with His incarnation, His miraculous works, His sinless life, His saving work on the cross and His resurrection. But this is not the end! After rising from the dead, Jesus appeared to His followers over a period of forty days and then ascended to heaven. There He was seated on a throne at His Father's right hand. All authority in heaven and on earth has been handed over by God the Father to the enthroned Jesus. There He remains. This means that in Jesus, God is ruling for us.

Note my words carefully. Jesus is not just reigning *over* us, but He is ruling *for* us! "God has put all things under the authority of Christ and has made him head over all things for the benefit of the church" (Eph. 1:22, NLT).

What is Jesus doing right now? He is ruling and praying. "Christ Jesus, who died—more than that, who was raised to life— is at the right hand of God and is also interceding for us" (Rom. 8:34). Jesus "is able to save completely those who come to God through him" precisely "because he always lives to intercede for them" (Heb. 7:25). Do you see the hope? Can you feel its power?

Writing Your Story

One of our primary goals has been to trace God's story from beginning to end, we are looking for the one thing God is doing through history. Our journey is not yet complete, but we have arrived at the center. The cross and resurrection of Jesus Christ are the joint events that create the hinge of all history. Everything that came before looked forward to this, and everything from here on out will look back to this. It stands to reason that if God's story turns on this hinge, then yours will too.

What do I mean?

As we considered seven reasons that Jesus is the perfect way for God to break His silence, did you notice anything different about the last one? The verb tense changed—from "was" to "is." Because Jesus rose and ascended and is now ruling in heaven for us, we must leave behind the past-tense verbs for present-tense verbs—we move from was to is! "Jesus Christ is the same yesterday and today and forever" (Heb. 13:8).

Far too often we substitute knowledge for experience. Many of us know what Jesus did but do not know Him in present, personal reality. It is possible that this chapter hasn't told you much you don't already know in terms of biblical knowledge. But I would like to ask you, Deep inside—in the core of your being—are the verbs you use to express what Christ has done simply past-tense ("was") or present-tense experience ("is")?

Jesus not just *was*, but *is* God's saving grace to us. Jesus *is* speaking to us. Jesus *is* dwelling among us. Jesus *is* working among us. Jesus *is* our righteousness. Jesus *is* redeeming us. Jesus *is* victorious for us. Jesus *is* ruling for us.

Jesus breaks the silence of God because He is God's grace and glory incarnate. God's grace is not a thing, a substance to be gained—God's grace is a Person to know and love and submit to and worship and serve. Jesus is God's saving grace; He is God's sanctifying grace; He is God's sustaining grace. Similarly, God's *glory* is not a thing—some ethereal, twilight-zone emanation. God's glory is Jesus. Jesus "is the radiance of God's glory" (Heb. 1:3). He, having been rejected again at His temple in Jerusalem, has built a new temple—your body (1 Cor. 6:19). If you open the door to Him in faith (Rev. 3:20), He will come and fill His temple!

Remember the plan of God is to take one man (Abraham) and make of Him one great nation (Israel) so that through that nation He might send one great Savior (Jesus) who might extend God's grace and demonstrate God's glory to all creation!

How is God doing in fulfilling His plan? Clearly He is right on course and right on time!

Remember, you are seeking your place in God's plan. You must understand something of God's story to find your story— and we are very close now to seeing the whole picture. But let me say this: As long as the verbs of your experience are simply past tense ("was"), you'll never really find your place in God's plan, because His intention is that you live in relationship with Him in the present. He wants to be personally present to guide the unfolding of your story.

Are you ready to meet Jesus here? Can you admit that He is speaking to you? Do you dare acknowledge that He wishes to dwell with you and to work in you? Will you allow Christ to be your righteousness before God? Will you name Him as your Redeemer? Are you willing to let Him live His life through you?

Why not schedule an uninterrupted, unhurried season of prayer alone with God so you can settle these matters before Him? Perhaps you want to keep this chapter open during your time of prayer so you can pray through each of the truths regarding what God has done and is doing for you through His Son Jesus. It is often helpful to write out a fresh prayer or covenant of trust with God at pivotal moments like these.

Reviewing God's Story

Take a few minutes now to review God's story as we understand it to this point. Be certain you can recall and understand the glorious saving grace God was and is pouring out through Jesus.

1. In Jesus, God was _____ to us.

2. In Jesus, God was _____ among us.

3. In Jesus, God was _____ among us.

4. In Jesus, God was _____ for us.

5. In Jesus, God was _____ us.

6. In Jesus, God was _____ for us.

7. In Jesus, God is _____ for us.

8. In short: Jesus is God's _____ and God's _____ incarnate!

Remembering God's Story

Scriptures	Matthew–John

Key Characters	John the Baptist, Jesus Christ, the disciples, Pharisees, Sadducees, Pilate, the Romans

Key Events	Jesus' birth, baptism by John, anointing by the Spirit, earthly ministry, Transfiguration, crucifixion, burial, resurrection, ascension

Key Verses	"You know . . . how God anointed Jesus of Nazareth with the Holy Spirit and power, and how he went around doing good and healing all who were under the power of the devil, because God was with him. . . . They killed him by hanging him on a tree, but God raised him from the dead on the third day and caused him to be seen." Acts 10:37–40

God's Story

Eternity Past

← Creation ⎫
          ⎬ Gen. 1–11
← Fall / Flood / Babel ⎭

2,000 yrs. {
← The Rise of Israel ⎫
          ⎬ Gen. 12–
← Temple ⚡ GLORY! ⎭ 1 Kings 10

400 yrs. {
← The Decline of Israel ⎫
          ⎬ 1 Kings 11
← Exile! → GLORY! ⎭ –2 Chron., Prov.

140 yrs. {
← Restoration of a Remnant ⎫ Ezra–
          ⎬ Esther,
          ⎭ Hag.–Mal.

400 yrs. {
← **400 Years of SILENCE!**

33 yrs. {
← ✝ ⎫ Matthew–
          ⎬ John

Eternity Future

Act II, Scene 2

A Seeking Grace
Acts–Jude

As most parents do, Julie and I told our children stories when they were small. We often recounted for them some exciting or humorous story from our past. Not infrequently, the story seemed so great to little ears that one of the kids would ask, "Where was *I* when that happened?"

We all want to be a part of a great story. We all long to be a part of *the* great story! Who doesn't long to understand where they fit? Who doesn't desire to have a share in God's great plan?

We have been seeking to understand history as God's story. The promise has been that as we understand His story, we are in a position to see and understand our own. But by now you may have begun to ask, where was *I* when all this happened?

We come now, at last, to our part in the unfolding of history. Let's make a run up to it so we can understand it well.

The curtain is about to open on Act II, Scene 2. God's plan has been to take one man (Abraham) and to make from him one great nation (Israel) so that through it God can provide one great Savior (Jesus) so that He might extend His grace and demonstrate His glory to all creation!

Let's take inventory of our progress.

One man? Abraham.

Check!

One great nation? Israel.

Check!

One great Savior? Jesus.

Check!

Grace extended and glory demonstrated to all creation?

Hmmm . . . wait a minute! His story is not done!

No, it is not. However, the scene about to unfold as the curtain rises again will show us just how God intends to complete this final step. And this is where you and I come in! As the curtain opens, a huge transition in this drama is about to take place. A major new character is going to be introduced. The changes will be so radical, so wholesale that it might seem that it's a different story. It might appear that an entirely new story has begun—but it hasn't. This transition will carry us all the way to the end, to the fulfillment of the plan.

Remember how God promised to resolve the story? Do you recall the goal appointed from the beginning? God said, "As I live, all the earth shall be filled with the glory of the LORD" (Num. 14:21, NKJV). Go back to the constants I told you about before we set out on this journey—determine never to lose sight of these two fixed points: Everything about everything is *about the glory of God*. Everything about everything is *by the grace of God*.

But just how does God plan to permeate all of creation with His grace and glory? Watch carefully now as the curtain rises before us!

A Transition Is Promised (Matthew 16:18)

Before Jesus died, rose and ascended, He spoke to His disciples about a transition to come. This transition would not be a new thing, but would be a shift in the one thing God had been about from eternity past.

When Jesus came to the region of Caesarea Philippi, he asked his disciples, "Who do people say the Son of Man is?" They replied, "Some say John the Baptist; others say Elijah; and still others, Jeremiah or one of the prophets." "But what about you?" he asked. "Who do you say I am?" Simon Peter answered, "You are the Christ, the Son of the living God." Jesus replied, "Blessed are you, Simon son of Jonah, for this was not revealed to you by man, but by my Father in heaven. And I tell you that you are Peter, and on this rock I will build my church, and the gates of Hades will not overcome it." (Matt. 16:13–18)

This is new! Here is the first mention of the church. In the entire Bible we have never heard mention of this before. What is this? It is a signal that a transition is coming.

Because Jesus told us this before His death, resurrection and ascension, we know that the formation of the church was not an afterthought. God did not say, "Oops, Israel rejected the Messiah! I've got to regroup! Initiate Plan B!"

No, this transition was in God's mind from the beginning. He just hadn't fully disclosed this part of His plan to His prophets. In fact, Paul calls the church a "mystery"—something previously hidden, but now made known (Eph. 3:2–9).

This message of Jesus to His disciples was His way of saying, "Watch for the transition! When the curtain opens on Act II, Scene 2, things will be different!"

Indeed, He immediately said to Peter, "I will give you the keys of the kingdom of heaven; whatever you bind on earth will be bound in heaven, and whatever you loose on earth will be loosed in heaven" (Matt. 16:19).

As this scene unfolds, don't take your eyes off Peter. He is going to unlock the doors of transition.

A Transmission Is Prescribed (Matthew 28:18–20)

What does "transmission" mean? Think of an automobile. The transmission is the part of the car that transmits the power from the engine to the axle. Without the transmission you would have no motion!

How do we get the grace and glory of God from a handful of disciples to all of creation? Remember, the goal is grace and glory to the whole earth (Num. 14:21)! So how do God's glory and grace go mobile?

We will discover that the transmission (the gear box that will transmit God's glory and grace to the world) is effected through a commission (a set of orders). In fact, so revolutionary is this transmission that we call it the Great Commission. A commission is defined as "a formal written warrant granting the power to perform various acts or duties" or the "authority to act for, in behalf of, or in place of another."[1]

This Great Commission is recorded in all four Gospels. Consider Matthew's version: "Then Jesus came to them and said, 'All authority in heaven and on earth has been given to me. Therefore go and make disciples of all nations, baptizing them in the name of the Father and of the Son and of the Holy Spirit, and teaching them to obey everything I have commanded you. And surely I am with you always, to the very end of the age" (28:18–20).

In this transfer of authority, Jesus issued one command: "Make disciples." This is the only imperative employed by the Savior here. He issued one order. But then He used three participles to describe the ways this commission was—and still is—to be carried out.

The first participle is "going." This tells us immediately that God's is a seeking grace! Jesus said, "The Son of Man came *to seek* and to save what was lost" (Luke 19:10). God's grace is never stagnant or sedentary. It is always in motion, always on the move. He is seeking, looking, searching and calling out in His grace.

It is difficult to estimate just how radical this shift is, as we'll see in the following paragraphs. We might liken it to the earth grinding to a halt on its axis and reversing the direction of its revolutions. Go plunge your hand in a tub of water and swirl it one direction. Then suddenly spin your hand the other way. Water flies everywhere! Eventually, of course, the vortex will begin moving in the opposite direction—but the initial change of course creates some waves.

Up until now God has localized the manifestation of His presence in one place (the temple in Jerusalem). Anyone wanting to be right with Him had been required to come to Jerusalem to offer sacrifices and be in His presence.

Even before the major transition God is making, Israel had been given a clear mission to the nations. God told Abram, "I will make you into a great nation . . . ; and all peoples on earth will be blessed through you" (Gen. 12:2–3). Isaiah and the Psalms speak often of this mission (see Isa. 42:6; 49:6; 51:4; 60:3; Ps. 67:1–7; 72:17–19; 98:2–3). But Israel's mission during these earlier generations might be succinctly stated as "Come and see!"

This is illustrated by a conversation Jesus once entered into with a Samaritan woman. He said to her, "Believe me, woman, a time is coming when you will worship the Father neither on this mountain nor in Jerusalem" (John 4:21). Jesus' words reveal that the Jews had been reared to believe that they and others who desired God's presence had to travel to the temple in Jerusalem. The Samaritans, on the other hand, had a similar belief about the mountain where their temple was located in Samaria. The transition ahead in God's plan would reveal that from here on out, both would be in error.

Now God was changing the entire orientation of the divine commission. No longer was it "Come and see!" Now the commission of God to His new people is "Go and tell!"

Sadly, many have understood Christianity as a practice of merely coming together in one place once a week rather than living a life on the go, in fellowship and on mission with Christ.

Equally sad is the fact that evangelism—carrying out our commission to make disciples—too often has been about dragging people into a church so the pastor can preach at them, instead of living in the power of the Spirit all week long and engaging people purposefully for Christ. When we live in this misunderstanding, we are living with an Old Testament mindset.

To "going," then, Jesus added "baptizing" (new believers giving a public testimony to their discipleship) and "teaching" (helping the believers with ongoing growth in their discipleship) as the means by which the Great Commission is to be completed.

When we live with this commission (reproducing disciples of Jesus Christ) in these ways (going, baptizing and teaching), we are slipping the automobile into gear. A transmission is taking place. Now we are poised to make progress toward God's goal! As we are true to our mission, then we are set to move with God in what He is doing in this world. But when we pursue our own agendas, we idle in neutral and go nowhere. We may roar and sound impressive, but we are left in the dust of history.

Now with the gears engaged, what else do we need? In a word, power!

The Transmission Is Powered (Acts 1:8)

There has to be power for a transmission to take place. Having set forth His commission (Luke 24:45–48), Jesus promised just such power: "I am going to send you what my Father has promised; but stay in the city until you have been clothed with power from on high" (24:49). The promise was fulfilled just a few days later:

> On one occasion, while he was eating with them, he gave them this command: "Do not leave Jerusalem, but wait for the gift my Father promised, which you have heard me speak about. For John baptized with water, but in a few days you will be baptized with the Holy Spirit." So when they met to-

gether, they asked him, "Lord, are you at this time going to restore the kingdom to Israel?" He said to them: "It is not for you to know the times or dates the Father has set by his own authority. But you will receive power when the Holy Spirit comes on you; and you will be my witnesses in Jerusalem, and in all Judea and Samaria, and to the ends of the earth." (Acts 1:4–8)

The Holy Spirit—the very Spirit of Jesus—is the power by which the fulfillment of God's eternal purpose will be accomplished. God will complete His plan through an inside-out work in His people!

Please understand. This is new. Jesus, the night before He died, spoke to His disciples about the Holy Spirit, saying, "You know him, for he lives with you and will be in you" (John 14:17). In the Old Testament the Spirit of God came upon individuals to empower them to do God's will at a particular time and place. But it does not seem to have been an abiding, indwelling relationship between the Holy Spirit and the person. All that, however, is about to change! For what do we discover in the very next chapter of Acts after Jesus told His disciples to wait for the promise? The Holy Spirit is given to God's people (Acts 2)!

So what is it that the Spirit brings to us?

Well, what are the two unchanging constants? They are, as by now we well know, grace and glory. As the church, we are Christ's *witnesses* (Acts 1:8)—and Jesus assured us that the *grace* (power) to fulfill this role will be ever available and always sufficient. As the church, we are Christ's *temple* (1 Cor. 3:16–17; 2 Cor. 6:16; Eph. 2:21)—and we are to house the *glory* of the indwelling Christ Himself! The God of glory and grace Himself inhabits us.

In Jesus the glory of God came back to the temple but departed once more because of the worldly practices taking place there. But now, at last, God's glory has come again to His temple—to His own people! To all of us together Paul asked, "Don't you know that you yourselves [plural] are God's temple and that God's Spirit lives in you?" (1 Cor. 3:16). To each of us individually he asked again, "Do you not know that your [singular] body is a temple of the Holy Spirit, who is in you, whom you have received from God?" (6:19).

Do you see it? The God of glory has returned to His temple! This is why God commands us: "Be filled with the Holy Spirit" (Eph. 5:18).

Of all the differences between New Testament and Old Testament living, perhaps the greatest difference is seen in this: we live in the age of the Spirit! But don't just take my word for it. Hear the apostle Paul!

> He has made us competent as ministers of a new covenant— not of the letter but of the Spirit; for the letter kills, but the Spirit gives life.
>
> Now if the ministry that brought death, which was engraved in letters on stone, came with glory, so that the Israelites could not look steadily at the face of Moses because of its glory, fading though it was, will not the ministry of the Spirit be even more glorious? If the ministry that condemns men is glorious, how much more glorious is the ministry that brings righteousness! For what was glorious has no glory now in comparison with the surpassing glory. And if what was fading away came with glory, how much greater is the glory of that which lasts!
>
> Therefore, since we have such a hope, we are very bold. We are not like Moses, who would put a veil over his face to keep the Israelites from gazing at it while the radiance was fading away. But their minds were made dull, for to this day the same veil remains when the old covenant is read. It has not been removed, because only in Christ is it taken away. Even to this day when Moses is read, a veil covers their hearts. But whenever anyone turns to the Lord, the veil is taken away. Now the Lord is the Spirit, and where the Spirit of the

Lord is, there is freedom. And we, who with unveiled faces all reflect the Lord's glory, are being transformed into his likeness with ever-increasing glory, which comes from the Lord, who is the Spirit. (2 Cor. 3:6–18)

Thus far we have a transition promised, a transmission pre-scribed and the transmission powered. But we haven't actually gone anywhere! So now you had best buckle up and hold on. Things are about to change!

The Transmission Is Produced (Acts 1–28)

The transmission is not just from God *to* us, but from God *through* us—to all creation! Just as Israel was chosen by God not as the end of His purposes but as a channel through which those purposes might be advanced, so too the church is chosen by God. The church itself is not the goal of all things, but the channel through which Christ will bring God's story to a grand culmination. We were never designed to be a cup, but a conduit. We are not a reservoir, but a river. We are not the end of God's grace—we are its pipeline to the entire world.

The Gospels of Matthew, Mark, Luke and John recount to us the history of Jesus' earthly ministry. The book of Acts then chronicles the history of what Jesus continued to do, which He was now accomplishing through His church. Luke began his second volume of history, Acts, by saying, "In my former book [the Gospel of Luke] . . . I wrote about all that Jesus *began* to do and to teach" (1:1). The clear implication is that the book of Acts is a record of what Jesus *continued* to do, but now through the disciples who He indwelt by His Spirit. So the book of Acts tells us how Christ produced this transmission through His church to the world.

The New Testament epistles of Romans through Jude pro-vide the teachings for the church as we go about Christ's mis-sion. These books of Scripture detail for us the "how" and "why" questions that arise as we labor to complete the commission Jesus has laid upon us. Seeing that these books of Scripture are not historical in nature and thus do not add directly to the storyline of what God is "doing" in the outworking of His plan, we simply point out their vital purpose, but leave their contents for you to examine in the light of this purpose.

There are several scriptural ways to track the advance of Christ through His church in the book of Acts. One way is *geographically*. Take a peek through the keyhole of Acts 1:8: "But you will receive power when the Holy Spirit comes on you; and you will be my witnesses in Jerusalem, and in all Judea and Samaria, and to the ends of the earth." Note the geographical markers the Spirit set forward at the start of this remarkable book and mission: Jerusalem (Acts 2–7), Judea/Samaria (Acts 8–12) and the ends of the earth (Acts 13–28).

Another way to track the advance of God's purpose in Acts is *biographically*. Acts 1–12 tells the story of the church through the life of Peter. Remember, I told you to keep your eyes on Peter! Then chapters 13–28 tell of the church's continuing advance through the life and ministry of the apostle Paul.

Yet another way of tracing the advance of God in Acts is *ethnically*. Acts 1–7 tells the story of the gospel first reaching the Jews. Acts 8–12 describes the gospel then progressing forward to both Jews and Gentiles. And from Acts 13 to the end of the book we see the gospel reaching more particularly to the Gentiles.

Do you recall how earlier in this scene we read that Peter had been given the "keys of the kingdom"? Did that make you scratch your head? The book of Acts explains just what Jesus meant by that expression. Peter was the apostle selected to open doors for an ethnic ministry transition from only Jews to all peoples. Who was it who preached on Pentecost? Peter (2:14–39). Who verified the message that had been preached to Samaritans? Peter (8:14–25). Who opened the door of faith to the Gentiles by proclaiming the gospel to a Gentile named Cornelius? Again, it was Peter (Acts 10)!

In fact, the last word of Peter in the book of Acts was, "Brothers, you know that some time ago God made a choice among you that the Gentiles might hear from my lips the message of the gospel and believe. . . . We believe it is through the grace of our Lord Jesus that we are saved, just as they are" (15:7, 11).

Take note! To the Jews Peter did not say, "Gentiles can be saved just as *we* are." No, he said, "We [Jews] are saved, just as *they* are"! No one—not Jews, not Gentiles; neither church folk, nor secularists—has a leg up on the grace of God. We all stand on level ground before the bar of God. We are all beggars of grace. Every one of us stands equally flummoxed before a holy God, and we are all equally dependent upon His salvation.

A final way of following the progress of God's purposes through the book of Acts is progressively. Luke, as he wrote the book of Acts, included a series of progress reports along the way. Note these markers:

> And the Lord added to their number daily those who were being saved. (2:47)

> So the word of God spread. The number of disciples in Jerusalem increased rapidly, and a large number of priests became obedient to the faith. (6:7)

> Then the church throughout Judea, Galilee and Samaria enjoyed a time of peace. It was strengthened; and encouraged by the Holy Spirit, it grew in numbers, living in the fear of the Lord. (9:31)

> But the word of God continued to increase and spread. (12:24)

> So the churches were strengthened in the faith and grew daily in numbers. (16:5)

> In this way the word of the Lord spread widely and grew in
> power. (19:20)

> For two whole years Paul stayed there in his own rented house
> and welcomed all who came to see him. Boldly and without
> hindrance he preached the kingdom of God and taught about
> the Lord Jesus Christ. (28:30–31)

The grace and glory of God were advancing not only geographically and progressively, but also culturally as God tran-
sitioned from a completely Jewish church to a largely Gentile
church. Why this cultural transition? Because the one divine
plan has always been aimed at "all creation"! God was never interested only in Israel. He loved Israel, to be sure. Yet His heart
was for Israel so that through them He might bring a Savior and
that through Him God's grace could be extended and His glory
demonstrated to all creation!

I invite you to notice how the book of Acts concludes. There
are twenty-eight chapters in this book, so go (at least in your
imagination) to the last of these with me.

There we find Paul under arrest in Rome. The Jewish leadership in that city came to see Paul soon after his captors had
brought him there. They wanted to understand the hubbub
about this apostle and the "sect" he left behind in every city he
visited. Paul "explained and declared to them the kingdom of
God and tried to convince them about Jesus from the Law of
Moses and from the Prophets" (28:23).

The result was that "some were convinced by what he said,
but others would not believe" (28:24). The leaders found themselves divided about Paul, and they determined to go their way.
As they did, Paul made one last statement:

> The Holy Spirit spoke the truth to your forefathers when he
> said through Isaiah the prophet: "Go to this people and say,
> 'You will be ever hearing but never understanding; you will

be ever seeing but never perceiving. For this people's heart has
become calloused; they hardly hear with their ears, and they
have closed their eyes. Otherwise they might see with their
eyes, hear with their ears, understand with their hearts and
turn, and I would heal them.'" Therefore I want you to know
that God's salvation has been sent to the Gentiles, and they
will listen! (28:25–28)

Understand, this parting salvo on the part of the apostle Paul
is the end of Scripture's historical record of the church. As the
back cover of the book of Acts is closed upon the pages of its
history, what is the posture of the church? What is the counte-
nance of the gospel's greatest missionary? Quite simply, it is this:
Forward to the ends of the earth!

The story of the church and of the advance of God's glory
and grace through the gospel of Jesus Christ simply rolls on. Its
persistent advance is untold in Scripture, but it is written (often
with the blood of its martyrs) across the pages of history in the
lives of generations of faithful disciples. These faithful men and
women transmit the gospel of glory and grace from one life to
another in an unending chain of Life that continues on—until
one day it will circle the globe and eventually include living links
from every "tribe and language and people and nation" (Rev.
5:9).

You might ask, but what about Israel? A full answer to that
question is beyond the scope of our present study. But I would
recommend a careful reading of Romans 9–11. There Paul tells
us how the glory and grace of God will yet be played out upon
the world stage through the Jewish people. There the apostle
concludes this line of reasoning by throwing his hands in the air
and shouting: "For from him and through him [this is grace!]
and to him are all things [this is glory!]." And he adds in exulta-
tion, "To him be the glory forever! Amen" (11:36).

But don't lose track of the book of Acts. Reflect again
upon how Luke concludes this scriptural history of the church.

Doesn't it seem strange that a book so well written, so compelling, so thoroughly researched, so clearly organized just kind of drops off without any real conclusion? Why would God do this?

He did it because the plan of God was not yet complete. The ends of the earth had not yet been reached! In one sense the book of Acts is still being written. You and I are living out *Acts 29*! The gospel is still advancing personally—one individual at a time. The gospel is going forward by life-to-life transference. We are living Acts 29! God is still writing the history of the church, not in infallible, inerrant Scripture—but through our lives on the pages of history.

Now don't miss this, please. The thing that got Israel in trouble was when they concluded God's grace was just for them. They enjoyed His grace, thinking somehow it was just about them. God has warned us Gentiles in the church that the danger of thinking that way exists for us as well: "They [Israel] were broken off because of unbelief, and you stand by faith. Do not be arrogant, but be afraid. For if God did not spare the natural branches, he will not spare you either" (Rom. 11:20–21).

We are in a dangerous place when we enjoy the grace of God simply for ourselves and think we are the goal of it all. When we live life on mission with God, keeping His plan and goal before us at all times, realizing that everything we have and are is given so that it can be poured back into His mission and plan, then we will continue to receive grace upon grace and will have His glory manifested in and through us.

The Transmission Is Perfected (Matthew 24:14)

How long is this advance to go on? Remember, God's goal is all creation! Jesus spoke of the terminus of the plan when He announced, "This gospel of the kingdom will be preached in the whole world as a testimony to all nations, and then the end will come" (Matt. 24:14).

At the dawn of the twentieth century, Albert Benjamin

Simpson, founder of the Christian and Missionary Alliance, was being greatly used of God and was seeing remarkable responses of sacrifice and faith to the message he proclaimed. The unbelieving world began to take notice. Reporters from secular newspapers began to investigate, skeptical of his intentions and his message. On one occasion, while Simpson was preaching on the Second Coming, one such reporter from the *New York Journal* approached him and asked, "Do you know when Christ will come?" He was baiting Simpson, hoping to lure him into unwisely setting a date for Christ's return.

But Simpson surprised the man by saying, "Yes. And I will tell you if you will promise to print just what I say, references and all." The reporter agreed eagerly. A.B. Simpson then quoted the words of Matthew 24:14. The reporter scribbled quickly to get every word. Simpson asked, "Have you written the reference?"

"Yes," came the reply, "what more?"

"Nothing more," said Simpson.

Laying aside his pencil, the reporter asked, "Do you mean to say you believe that when the gospel has been preached to all nations, Jesus will return?"

"Just that," came Simpson's reply.

Suddenly a knowing look washed over the reporter's face, and the newly enlightened man replied, "Then I think I begin to see daylight." He added, "I see the motive and the motive-power in this movement."

Before their parting, Simpson told him, "You see more than some of the doctors of divinity."[2]

Don't be offended, please—but I must ask, what if we actually believed all this?

Would you look at your neighbor differently? Would you use your resources differently? Would you raise your kids differently? Would you head off to work differently each morning?

Peter believed it. The same Peter used of God to open the

door for the gospel's entrance into the Gentile world wrote to people just like you and me asking, "What kind of people ought you to be? You ought to live holy and godly lives as you look forward to the day of God *and speed its coming*" (2 Pet. 3:11–12). Think of it! The way you and I live, the kinds of things we do with the grace God extends to us can hasten the return of Jesus Christ. Amazing!

Writing My Story

So far at the end of each study, the curtain has closed and the scene has come to an end. But don't miss the difference here: *the curtain is still up on Act II, Scene 2!* You and I are onstage. Your story is being written even as God's story unfolds on the stage of human history.

We're about to discover, in the final act, how God's story (and ours) ends! Then we'll have one more study to help you locate your story in the midst of the one God is writing. But, in anticipation of that moment, let me provide you here with several keys to understanding your story.

Don't just read the following statements; take some time to wait over them. Turn them over in your mind. Fashion them into a filter through which you mentally pour your thoughts, activities, direction, motivation and the whole pattern and substance of your life. Transform them into a season of extended prayer with God. Be sure to listen for (and jot down) the things He impresses upon your heart and mind as you wait before Him.

Though you may not be ready to draw final conclusions about what your story should be, so far we have discovered this about God's story, and yours:

1. Your story is not about you—it's about the glory of God.
2. Your story will not be written in your strength—but by the grace of God.

3. Your story is part of something that will last—from eternity to eternity!

4. Your story is part of an anthology—the more you help other people write their story, the better yours turns out.

5. You are not the central character in your story—God is.

6. Finally, your story matters—strategically and eternally!

Reviewing God's Story

Take a few moments to review the progress of God's story as He seeks to extend His grace and magnify His glory to the ends of the earth.

1. A transition is _____. (Matt. 16:18)

2. A transmission is _____. (Matt. 28:18–20)

3. The transmission is _____. (Acts 1:8)

4. The transmission is _____. (Acts 1–28)

> Geographically (Acts 1:8)
> > Jerusalem (Acts 2–7)
> > Judea and Samaria (Acts 8–12)
> > Ends of the earth (Acts 13–28)
> Biographically
> > Peter (Acts 1–12)
> > Paul (Acts 13–28)
> Ethnically
> > The gospel goes to Jews (Acts 1–7)
> > The gospel goes to Jews and Gentiles (Acts 8–12)
> > The gospel goes to Gentiles (Acts 13–28)
> Progressively
> > Acts 2:47
> > Acts 6:7
> > Acts 9:31
> > Acts 12:24
> > Acts 28:30–31

Personally
"Acts 29"

5. The transmission is _____. (Matt. 24:14)

Remembering God's Story

Scriptures	Acts–Jude

Key Characters	Peter, John, Stephen, James, Paul, you and me!

Key Events	Jesus' ascension, Pentecost, Peter's ministry, Stephen and James the first martyrs, Paul's missionary travels, the gospel to the ends of the earth!

Key Verse	"But you will receive power when the Holy Spirit comes on you; and you will be my witnesses in Jerusalem, and in all Judea and Samaria, and to the ends of the earth." Acts 1:8

God's Story

Eternity Past

← Creation

← Fall / Flood / Babel } Gen. 1–11

2,000 yrs. {
← The Rise of Israel

← Temple ⚡ **GLORY!** } Gen. 12– 1 Kings 10

400 yrs. {
← The Decline of Israel

← Exile! → **GLORY!** } 1 Kings 11 –2 Chron., Prov.

140 yrs. {
← Restoration of a Remnant } Ezra– Esther, Hag.–Mal.

400 yrs. {
← **400 Years of SILENCE!**

33 yrs. {
← ✝ } Matthew– John

? yrs. {
← Great Commission

← Pentecost ⚡ **Spirit given!**

← Antioch Church

← Paul's Missionary journeys

← **Acts 29:** You & Me! } Acts– Jude

Eternity Future

Act III

A Realized Grace
Revelation

A story has long been told of a great composer whose heart was broken by a rebellious son. The son routinely came in late at night, after his father and mother had already retired to their room for a night's rest. But the son, knowing his father's nature, would find his way to the piano before he finally went to bed. There he would methodically and with great volume play seven simple notes of the scale on the piano, but he always left the eighth and crowning note unplayed. Having struck the seventh note, he would make his way to his room with a smug satisfaction.

The composer-father, from within his room, could hear the notes being sounded. He would listen to them one by one, unconsciously counting them off. Yet there was something unresolved, something left hanging. He kept waiting for that eighth note to be sounded. He would lie in his bed, trying to ignore the omission. But the longer he lay there—the longer the octave hung unresolved in midair—the more uncomfortable the musician always became. Finally, unable to stand it any longer, the great composer would throw back the covers, storm out of his room, march down the stairs, make his way to the piano and, with one finger, strike the last and resolving note of the octave scale.[1] Then his heart could finally be at rest.

Do you feel a bit like that composer? So many notes have been played on the keys of humanity throughout history, yet there is something left unresolved, some note that simply must be sounded before our hearts can be at rest. Actually, the seventh note of the major scale is called the "leading note." It is so called because it naturally leads to the next crowning and completing note. Nothing is complete without that eighth note. No one can rest until the final note is sounded.

Have you ever wondered how it is that we know when to applaud during a symphony? We usually don't think about when to applaud—it just happens; we just know it is time. We know because something has resolved. There are moments of silence along the way, but we know not to clap at those times. Why? How do we know? Because those are discordant pauses; the music has not been resolved. When the final note is sounded, we know it; our hearts leap with appreciation and our hands meet together in applause!

We want to see this plan, the eternal plan of God, come together. To this point in our journey, we have been observing God's story in history. It has been a matter of facts, time and space, events, people, nations, etc. But in our last study we came to Act II, Scene 2 and noted that even now, the curtain is still up and the drama still unfolding. Though the chapter closed and the study concluded, the act and the scene are still being played out. You and I are on the stage, living out the rest of the story.

But how does the plan come together? How does it resolve? When will it be time for applause?

To answer these questions our perspective must change. We are about to transition from history to prophecy.

That is not the same as transitioning from fact to fiction. No, we aren't moving from certainty to speculation. Don't forget that much of what lies behind us as history was once spoken as prophecy as well. And it has been fulfilled—perfectly. But here is the big challenge: while looking backward at history, we can see that God has proven one-hundred-percent accurate in His prophecies to this point—but it is equally true that the details are a lot easier to make out in the rearview mirror than they are through the windshield. That is to say—fulfilled prophecy is easier to understand than is as-yet-to-be-fulfilled prophecy.

When Jesus came the first time, He came in fulfillment of prophecy. His life was the unfolding of prophetic Scripture. But it seems that no one, not even the most faithful of His followers, understood exactly how it would all take place, though they had pored over the Scriptures their whole lives. Yet when Jesus was born and as He lived out His life, people could see that it happened just as it had been spoken.

I suspect that is how it will be with Christ's Second Advent as well. Thus, I suggest that two things will prove true from this point on in our journey. First, everything God has prophesied will come true, to the detail. Second, not everything about those details is as clear now as it will be one day. Thus, while the curtain is still up on Act II, Scene 2 and we are busying ourselves with taking the gospel of God's glory and grace in Christ to the ends of the earth, let's allow ourselves to look ahead to the final act of God's story (and ours!)—Act III. Because, after all, our hearts will all leap with applause when God sounds the final note!

A Hope Worth Holding Onto

As the end of this divine drama draws near, don't cringe in fear and peek through just one clenched eyelid. Our hope is twofold, and looking through both eyes of faith brings that hope into three-dimensional reality.

Ours is a *hope of grace.* "Therefore, prepare your minds for action; be self-controlled; set your hope fully on the grace to be given you when Jesus Christ is revealed" (1 Pet. 1:13).

But someone objects, "What do you mean, *hope* of grace? Haven't we already received grace?" Yes, of course we have. But we shall have it more fully. It will be a *realized* grace! We already enjoy a standing in God's grace (Rom. 5:2), but one day we shall be thrown into an *ocean* of grace! Indeed, Peter calls our Lord "the God of all grace, who called you to his eternal glory in Christ" (1 Pet. 5:10).

Ours is also a *hope of glory*. Please allow the following words to be like a gentle waterfall washing over you. This hope of glory is the call of salvation: through Christ "we have gained access by faith into this *grace* in which we now stand. And we rejoice in the hope of the *glory* of God" (Rom. 5:2). The grace of the past and the glory of the future are connected! We know that because "those he predestined, he also called; those he called, he also justified; those he justified, he also *glorified*" (8:30).

This hope of glory sustains us in our suffering: "I consider that our present sufferings are not worth comparing with the *glory* that will be revealed in us" (Rom. 8:18). Paul insisted that "our light and momentary troubles are achieving for us an eternal *glory* that far outweighs them all" (2 Cor. 4:17). Peter contended that trials come to you "so that your faith . . . may be proved genuine and may result in praise, *glory* and honor when Jesus Christ is revealed" (1 Pet. 1:7). He exhorted, "Rejoice that you participate in the sufferings of Christ, so that you may be overjoyed when his *glory* is revealed" (1 Pet. 4:13). This all takes place "that He might present to Himself the church in all her *glory*" (Eph. 5:27, NASB).

And this hope of glory holds us in suspense: in this present age we are "looking for the blessed hope and the appearing of the *glory* of our great God and Savior, Christ Jesus" (Titus 2:13, NASB). When He comes again, Christ "will transform the body of our humble state into conformity with the body of His *glory*" (Phil. 3:21, NASB). And "when Christ, who is your life, appears, then you also will appear with him in *glory*" (Col. 3:4). Peter described himself as "one who also will share in the *glory* to be revealed" (1 Pet. 5:1).

And finally, this hope of glory calls us to faithfulness: the essence of hell is to be placed "away from the presence of the Lord and from the *glory* of His power" (2 Thess. 1:9, NASB). Yet God "is able to keep you from stumbling, and to make you stand in the presence of His *glory* blameless with great joy" (Jude 24, NASB).

Events Worth Watching Out For

Thus, I invite you to watch for several prophetic events as you head down the highway of life—remembering that prophetic fulfillments are always clearer than prophetic utterances, that things are more obvious when viewed in the rearview mirror rather than through the windshield.

Some time back our family was returning from a wedding which had taken place several hours' drive from our home. The clock on the dashboard was about to roll over to midnight on that dark Saturday night. My wife and three children were asleep, and I was fighting not to join them in that state as I guided our car toward home.

Driving at such a late hour, when darkness is engulfing everything and sleep pulling at my eyelids, sometimes I find it difficult to distinguish the various lights from one another. On this particular occasion, my family and I were out in the countryside on an interstate highway. Traffic was sparse, but there were several lights headed toward me—on the other side of the interstate, of course. Or so I thought.

In that slumping stupor I suddenly realized that a pair of those lights was on our side of the interstate—headed straight for us! In the same instant that I realized its presence, the car was upon us. It had to have been traveling in the vicinity of a hundred miles per hour as it tore past us in the left lane. I didn't realize the presence of the car until it was about a half second from what could have been impact.

It had been only moments before that I had leisurely moved

into the left lane to pass a slower vehicle. I had only recently returned to the right lane—and out of the oncoming car's path. By the time I released some incoherent cry in response to the danger, the car's taillights were tiny dots in my rearview mirror, about to disappear into the darkness behind me. I cried out, "That guy's going the wrong direction down the interstate!" As my bleary-eyed family raised their heads, they awakened to the reality that had nearly been ours.

Remember, Peter commanded us to "prepare [our] minds for action" (1 Pet. 1:13). We need to be watching through the darkness—looking for the glory and grace to be brought us when Christ returns.

We don't yet have the luxury of viewing these prophetic events through the insight of hindsight. So may I issue a word of caution for you to heed as we watch eagerly for them to be fulfilled? Here it is: don't love a prophetic chronology more than you love your coming King! Jesus specifically told us no one knows when He will return—not even Him! "No one knows about that day or hour, not even the angels in heaven, nor the Son, but only the Father" (Matt. 24:36). Yet we are told to watch; and to do so eagerly! "Watch therefore, for you do not know what hour your Lord is coming" (24:42, NKJV).

This then brings us to the book of Revelation. Remember, we're watching this through the windshield. We don't have all the insight of hindsight. Revelation is a book of great mystery and debate. Someone has wisely said that its opening and closing chapters are abundantly clear: Revelation 1–5 plainly shows that God is on the throne, sovereign and keeping His own! Likewise, Revelation 17–22 clearly reveals evil as being defeated and Christ coming in victory to reign with His church. It is the chapters in the middle of the book that are of greatest debate. For this reason, let's keep our major focus on the parts that are clearest.

There are seven events foretold in Scripture on which we need to keep our spiritual eyes sharply focused. These events march us toward the culmination of God's great plan, the very plan established in eternity past and to be enjoyed throughout eternity future. Thus, living in this critical hour, we need to ask God for clarity of spiritual sight to see these events as they unfold.

The Rapture. "For the Lord himself will come down from heaven, with a loud command, with the voice of the archangel and with the trumpet call of God, and the dead in Christ will rise first. After that, we who are still alive and are left will be caught up together with them in the clouds to meet the Lord in the air. And so we will be with the Lord forever" (1 Thess. 4:16–17). "Listen, I tell you a mystery: We will not all sleep, but we will all be changed—in a flash, in the twinkling of an eye, at the last trumpet. For the trumpet will sound, the dead will be raised imperishable, and we will be changed" (1 Cor. 15:51–52).

But when will this happen? That has always been the big question. Will the rapture take place before the tribulation? Or in the middle? Or at the end of the tribulation?

These are not unimportant questions. Unfortunately, a full investigation is beyond the scope of our present work. So let me simply ask, what did Paul call the rapture? He dubbed it "a mystery." He did so for good reason. After thousands of years and multiplied generations of biblical scholarship, church history proves that Paul named it correctly at the beginning. The great news we *do* have about the rapture is simply this: It will happen! Its timing is not unimportant, but it would seem that its timing is not as clearly revealed as its reality. And I reissue my warning: Don't love a chronology more than your King! Paul speaks of those "who have loved His appearing" (2 Tim. 4:8, NASB). Are you among them? Don't fall in love with being "right" more than you love the Righteous One and the hope of His coming.

Having established this perspective in our minds, there are nevertheless other events to come which the Scriptures describe. As history moves toward its climax, we can expect to see some evidence of these things approaching. The following are events worth watching for on the horizon of history.

The Tribulation. This time of intense, worldwide suffering seems to be described for us in Revelation 6–18. It will be a time when seals are broken, trumpets sounded and bowls full of wrath emptied upon the earth. This will be a time of unmatched suffering for the entire earth. This will be a season of judgment against all sin.

But the Tribulation will also serve a specific purpose as it relates to Israel. It is referred to in the Old Testament as the "time of Jacob's trouble" (Jer. 30:7, NKJV). The prophet Daniel's seventieth week will finally come about, and it will result in "shattering the power of the holy people" (Dan. 12:7, NASB). God will use the Tribulation to destroy Israel's dependence on herself and prepare her to receive her King, Jesus.

Even as the holiness of God's glory is being demonstrated through His judgment against sin, He will still demonstrate grace. In history's darkest hour both glory and grace will still reign! Through His prophet God said, "I will pour out on the house of David and the inhabitants of Jerusalem *a spirit of grace* and supplication. They will look on me, the one they have pierced, and they will mourn for him as one mourns for an only child, and grieve bitterly for him as one grieves for a firstborn son" (Zech. 12:10).

The Battle of Armageddon. The Tribulation will ultimately result in a horrific, epic battle known as Armageddon. In a final display of arrogant blasphemy, the antichrist (the beast) will rally the unbelieving world against Israel, intent upon her total annihilation:

> Then I saw the beast and the kings of the earth and their armies gathered together to make war against the rider on the horse and his army. But the beast was captured, and with him the false prophet who had performed the miraculous signs on

his behalf. With these signs he had deluded those who had received the mark of the beast and worshiped his image. The two of them were thrown alive into the fiery lake of burning sulfur. The rest of them were killed with the sword that came out of the mouth of the rider on the horse, and all the birds gorged themselves on their flesh. (Rev. 19:19–21)

The Return of Christ. Just when Israel seems destined for utter destruction, her Messiah, Jesus Christ, will return to earth. Jesus Himself said, "At that time the sign of the Son of Man will appear in the sky, and all the nations of the earth will mourn. They will see the Son of Man coming on the clouds of the sky, with power and great glory" (Matt. 24:30). On another occasion He promised, "The Son of Man is going to come in his Father's glory with his angels, and then he will reward each person according to what he has done" (16:27). The apostle John reported:

> I saw heaven standing open and there before me was a white horse, whose rider is called Faithful and True. With justice he judges and makes war. His eyes are like blazing fire, and on his head are many crowns. He has a name written on him that no one knows but he himself. He is dressed in a robe dipped in blood, and his name is the Word of God. The armies of heaven were following him, riding on white horses and dressed in fine linen, white and clean. Out of his mouth comes a sharp sword with which to strike down the nations. 'He will rule them with an iron scepter.' He treads the winepress of the fury of the wrath of God Almighty. On his robe and on his thigh he has this name written: KING OF KINGS AND LORD OF LORDS. (Rev. 19:11–16)

The Millennium. Upon His return to earth and His triumphant victory over His earthly enemies, Jesus Christ will establish His rule upon and over the whole earth and its inhabitants. When He was on earth the first time, Jesus promised, "When the Son of Man comes in his glory, and all the angels with him, he will sit on his throne in heavenly glory" (Matt. 25:31). The scene painted in Revelation is gripping:

> And I saw an angel coming down out of heaven, having the key to the Abyss and holding in his hand a great chain. He seized the dragon, that ancient serpent, who is the devil, or Satan, and bound him for a thousand years. He threw him into the Abyss, and locked and sealed it over him, to keep him from deceiving the nations anymore until the thousand years were ended. After that, he must be set free for a short time. I saw thrones on which were seated those who had been given authority to judge. And I saw the souls of those who had been beheaded because of their testimony for Jesus and because of the word of God. They had not worshiped the beast or his image and had not received his mark on their foreheads or their hands. They came to life and reigned with Christ a thousand years. (The rest of the dead did not come to life until the thousand years were ended.) This is the first resurrection. Blessed and holy are those who have part in the first resurrection. The second death has no power over them, but they will be priests of God and of Christ and will reign with him for a thousand years. (20:1–6)

During this one-thousand-year era, Satan will be bound while Christ reigns on earth from Jerusalem. The nation of Israel will be restored. All the divine promises to her, found in the Old Testament, will be literally and completely fulfilled as God vindicates His faithfulness. It is even said that the saints of God are to rule with Christ.

But why this one-thousand-year earthly reign? Some say the millennium is merely a "spiritual reign" taking place presently in the hearts of those who know Christ by faith. What is the need for a literal, earthly kingdom?

The answer is, quite simply, to fulfill completely the appointed goal of God. That goal has always been to take one man

(Abraham) and make from him one great nation (Israel) so that through it He might provide one great Savior (Jesus) who will extend God's grace and demonstrate God's glory to all creation. Without such a literal, earthly reign of Christ, vast landscapes of God's promises to Israel would go unfulfilled! Why a literal, earthly kingdom? Because God's purposes and promises demand it!

The Great White Throne. At the conclusion of the millennial reign of Christ will come what the Bible calls the judgment at the Great White Throne:

> Then I saw a great white throne and him who was seated on it. Earth and sky fled from his presence, and there was no place for them. And I saw the dead, great and small, standing before the throne, and books were opened. Another book was opened, which is the book of life. The dead were judged according to what they had done as recorded in the books. The sea gave up the dead that were in it, and death and Hades gave up the dead that were in them, and each person was judged according to what he had done. Then death and Hades were thrown into the lake of fire. The lake of fire is the second death. If anyone's name was not found written in the book of life, he was thrown into the lake of fire. (20:11–15)

Following this judgment there will be only two divisions of reality: heaven or hell! The Great White Throne will be a time of judgment, not for believers, but for those who have persisted in rebellious unbelief. Those who have trusted in Christ have already seen their sins judged at the cross, in Christ. Our sins were judged there "once for all" (Heb. 9:12; 10:10). They were judged eternally in Christ, so that we will not and cannot be condemned for them. But for those who have not repented and believed in Christ, this Great White Throne should be, and will become, their greatest terror.

The eternal state. For those not condemned at the Great

White Throne—that is to say, for all those who pass from this life having repented and placed their faith in the Lord Jesus Christ—eternity will be full of conscious, joyful bliss. This eternal state will entail a new heaven and a new earth (Rev. 21–22). Indeed, that city of our eternal dwelling is to be called the New Jerusalem.

In that day God Himself will declare, "It is done" (21:6)! Reflect upon that for a moment. Read those three words in the context of our entire pursuit of understanding God's story. Finally, that which God set in motion, way back in the dark, misty mystery of the divine counsels in eternity past, will find its ultimate and complete fulfillment! God Himself prepares to reach down and sound the final, resolving note of His story. Know this: a time is coming when God will finally assert, "It is done."

And notice the next words God will utter. "I am the Alpha and the Omega, the Beginning and the End" (21:6). God says, "I am out of eternity past and continue to live unceasingly through all time and throughout eternity future!" I predate all things, and all things will find their continued, eternal existence in Me!"

And what have been the two fixed constants from the very beginning? Will they be found when God's plan comes to fruition? Listen to the apostle John's report:

> And he carried me away in the Spirit to a mountain great and high, and showed me the Holy City, Jerusalem, coming down out of heaven from God. It shone with the glory of God, and its brilliance was like that of a very precious jewel, like a jasper, clear as crystal. . . . I did not see a temple in the city, because the Lord God Almighty and the Lamb are its temple. The city does not need the sun or the moon to shine on it, for the glory of God gives it light, and the Lamb is its lamp. The nations will walk by its light, and the kings of the earth will bring their splendor into it. On no day will its gates ever be

shut, for there will be no night there. The glory and honor of the nations will be brought into it. (21:10–11, 22–26)

What would you call that? GLORY!

What was the other fixed constant? Will it be found when all history has been proven to be His story?

Then the angel showed me the river of the water of life, as clear as crystal, flowing from the throne of God and of the Lamb down the middle of the great street of the city. On each side of the river stood the tree of life, bearing twelve crops of fruit, yielding its fruit every month. And the leaves of the tree are for the healing of the nations. No longer will there be any curse. The throne of God and of the Lamb will be in the city, and his servants will serve him. They will see his face, and his name will be on their foreheads. There will be no more night. They will not need the light of a lamp or the light of the sun, for the Lord God will give them light. And they will reign for ever and ever. (22:1–5)

What would you call that? GRACE! Amazing grace!

It is true. It has always been true. It will ever be true: everything about everything is *always about* the glory of God! And everything about everything is *always by* the grace of God! In that day the old hymn will be truer than ever: "The things of [this present] earth will grow strangely dim, in the light of His *glory* and *grace*." Our hearts will leap, and we will lift our hands to begin the eternal applause . . .

But wait. There is one more thing.

An End Worth Holding Out For

We've covered a great deal of ground in the few short scenes of this book. We've spanned the distance from eternity to eternity! I have attempted to go quickly enough so that you don't lose the clear line of the one thing God's been unfolding in history, but slowly enough to make sure you understand this plan at each point along the way. But now we come to *"the end"* (1 Cor. 15:24).

Ask yourself, When its all been said and done, what will things be like? Tough question, isn't it? Carefully scan these words of the apostle Paul, for they contain the answer:

> Then the end will come, when he [Jesus] hands over the kingdom to God the Father after he has destroyed all dominion, authority and power. For he must reign until he has put all his enemies under his feet. The last enemy to be destroyed is death. For he "has put everything under his feet." Now when it says that "everything" has been put under him, it is clear that this does not include God himself, who put everything under Christ. When he has done this, then the Son himself will be made subject to him who put everything under him, so that God may be all in all. (1 Cor. 15:24–28)

By now we should understand that history is linear, not cyclical.[2] That is to say, it moves in a line from a beginning to an end. We are not caught in an unending loop of bad reruns from the past. We are headed somewhere—*everything* is headed somewhere! There is coming a time, in "the end," when the authority invested in Christ by the Father will be brought to its end goal. The kingdom of God will win. Justice will be served. All "dominion, authority and power" will be destroyed. Christ will be Victor! Finally and forever, all that displeases and dishonors God will be under His feet!

Having won the war He was sent into, Jesus will hand the kingdom over to the Father once again: He then "will be made subject to him who put everything under him" (15:28). Think of it! How can the co-eternal, co-equal Son eternally subject Himself to the Father with whom He shares all the essence and prerogatives of deity?

A.T. Robertson is both succinct and accurate on this point: "The passage is a summary of mysteries which our present knowledge does not enable us to explain, and which our present faculties, perhaps, do not enable us to understand."[3]

But though we cannot entirely wrap our minds around it, Jesus' subjection to His Father infers no inferiority of the Son to the Father either in His person, nature or dignity. It simply means that even the Son, without surrendering His deity or dignity, is willing to submit Himself eternally to the Father so that the authority of the triune God might be forever a wonder that the new creation can't stop gazing upon!

When these unsearchable events have played themselves out, then God will be "all in all." The end goal of all history—from eternity past to eternity future—will have been achieved! God will be seen clearly as the source from which all things flow, the channel through which all things arrive and the goal toward which all things advance (Rom. 11:36). This has been the target from before time: "As I live, all the earth will be filled with the glory of the Lord" (Num. 14:21, NASB). "Praise be to his glorious name forever; may the whole earth be filled with his glory" (Ps. 72:19). "For the earth will be filled with the knowledge of the glory of the Lord, as the waters cover the sea" (Hab. 2:14). "The Lord will be king over the whole earth. On that day there will be one Lord, and his name the only name" (Zech. 14:9). And so we pray, "Let your glory be over all the earth" (Ps. 57:5, 11; 108:5, ESV).

Know this: a time is coming when the sound of countless millions, yea, billions, of knees hitting the dust in humble submission to Christ will be heard (Phil. 2:10–11). Some will bend their knees willingly, having prepared for that day in countless times of personal worship during their sojourn on earth. They will bend low in joy as they give glory to Christ and will pass into a life of bliss forever in the presence of their Savior and Lord. Others will find unyielding knees buckled under the sheer weight of the awesome unveiled glory of God in Christ! Having never acknowledged Christ in this life, they will find they can do no other than bow in worship before Him then. Theirs will be a parting admission of His rightful place, even as they pass out of His presence forever into eternal torment. Either way, all will bow.

Likewise, we are told that every tongue will utter the confession, "Jesus Christ is Lord" (Phil. 2:11). They will do so "to the glory of God the Father"! For some it will be the sweet, resounding echoes of their heart's song, which was sung through difficult days as they journeyed through this life. Their song of earthly praise will become an eternal one of heavenly worship. Others will force the words over lips that have refused to honor Christ for a lifetime. Even as they clench their teeth and their eyes begin to weep, void of any hope or comfort throughout eternity, they will utter the words they resisted so long: "Jesus Christ is Lord"!

With all humanity recognizing Him for who He is and all created beings looking on, Jesus will then take His place in glad submission to the Father—the brilliant light of His glorious Person becoming the perpetual lamp of the New Jerusalem. Then will the eternal goal of the triune God be realized. God will be, by means of His grace and with a view to His glory, "all in all."

From across the landscape of human history, every stream of events is being divinely drawn, collecting in the trickles and creek beds of time and space, gathering in the brooks and streams of individuals' and families' lives, pouring together into the rivers of cultures and nations. All these events are rushing toward a culminating confluence of triumph in which the wonder of God's grace and the universal demonstration of God's glory will thunder forth forever!

Hush! Be still! This is holy ground. Pause and worship Him!

This is God's story! This is His story. This will be history. Now, may I ask the one question that lingers, begging for an answer? What is your story? Where will you be found when everything is said and done? Where will you be found in relationship to the God of glory and grace?

> There is a definite goal toward which history is progressing. History is not, then, merely chance happenings. And the force causing its movement is not impersonal atoms or blind fate. It is, rather, a loving God with whom we can have a personal relationship. We may look forward with assurance, then, toward the attainment of the *telos* of the universe. And we may align our lives with what we know will be the outcome of history.[4]

Do you remember where we began this journey? Determine now never to lose sight of that final, climactic image of eternity's advent that we looked at from the *Chronicles of Narnia*. It is truer where we stand now than ever before:

> The things that began to happen after that were so great and beautiful that I cannot write them. And for us this is the end of all the stories. . . . But for them it was only the beginning of the real story. All their life in this world and all their adventures in Narnia had only been the cover and the title page: now at last they were beginning Chapter One of the Great Story which no one on earth has read: which goes on for ever: in which every chapter is better than the one before.[5]

Writing My Story

I say it again: this is a holy moment! The final resolving note of history's symphony has just been sounded. Be still in God's presence. Don't rush. Linger here. In the midst of the events described in the book of Revelation, it says, "There was silence in heaven for about half an hour" (8:1). Silence might be a wise course for us now as well.

Move now to expressions of worship. Applaud your Savior

with words of adoration and praise. Exalt Him in His glory. Give Him thanks for His grace.

In our next study we will devote ourselves entirely to determining how all of this wonderful perspective on God's story enables each of us to find our own story. Nothing will prepare you better for that study than a season of praise and thanksgiving in the presence of God. Do that now. Do it well—extolling God's glory and enjoying His grace.

Reviewing God's Story

Before you move on, see if you can recount the seven key events for which we should watch the horizon:

1. _____

2. _____

3. _____

4. _____

5. _____

6. _____

7. _____

Remembering God's Story

Scriptures	Revelation

Key Characters	Jesus, the church, Israel, the antichrist!

Key Events	Rapture, Tribulation, Armageddon, Second Coming, Millennium, Great White Throne, eternal state

Key Verses	"Then the end will come, when he hands over the kingdom to God the Father after he has destroyed all dominion, authority and power. For he must reign until he has put all his enemies under his feet. . . . It is clear that this does not include God himself, who put everything under Christ. When he has done this, then the Son himself will be made subject to him who put everything under him, so that God may be all in all."
	1 Corinthians 15:24–25, 27–28

God's Story

Eternity Past

← Creation ⎫
← Fall / Flood / Babel ⎬ Gen. 1–11

2,000 yrs. ⎧ ← The Rise of Israel ⎫ Gen. 12–
       ⎩ ← Temple ⚡ **GLORY!** ⎬ 1 Kings 10

400 yrs. ⎧ ← The Decline of Israel ⎫ 1 Kings 11
       ⎨   ⎬ –2 Chron.,
       ⎩ ← Exile! → **GLORY!**   ⎭ Prov.

140 yrs. ⎰ ← Restoration of a Remnant ⎫ Ezra–
                                       ⎬ Esther,
                                       ⎭ Hag.–Mal.

400 yrs. ⎰ ← :400 Years of SILENCE!:

33 yrs. ⎰ ← ✝ ⎱ Matthew– John

← Great Commission ⎫
← Pentecost ⚡ **Spirit given!** ⎬
← Antioch Church   ⎬ Acts– Jude
← Paul's Missionary journeys ⎬
← **Acts 29:** You & Me!   ⎭

? yrs.

← 2nd Coming of Christ! ⎫
← 1,000 yr. reign of Christ ⎬ Revelation
← Great White Throne Judgment ⎬
← New Heavens & New Earth ⎭

Eternity Future

PART 3

MY STORY

To be a person is to have a story.
—**William Bausch**

Throughout history, truth has been considered a form of dementia, and those who have turned away from fantasy and fixed their eyes on reality, judged insane.
—**Malcolm Muggeridge**

I believe in Christianity as I believe that the sun has risen: not only because I see it, but because by it I can see everything else.
—**C.S. Lewis**

DISCOVERING YOUR STORY

A Personal Grace

What if you discovered that what you thought was the story of your life really wasn't? At least, not entirely.

That is precisely what happened to Elyse Schein and Paula Bernstein. Both women had learned at an early age that they had been adopted. What they had never been told was that somewhere out there, each of them had an identical twin. The two girls had been separated at birth and adopted by different families. They had even been, for a time, a part of a special study that observed the effects of identical twins being separated from one another. Again, they had no idea that they were being studied. Eventually, however, as adults, they found their way to the larger story and, in the end, to one another. Their story is recounted in their book *Identical Strangers*.[1]

The fact is that most of us live our lives with only a partial understanding of our whole story. I'm not suggesting that you may have an identical twin wandering amid the world's billions of people. I am reminding you that your story is intricately tied to God's story—and most people never make the connection between theirs and His. But you wouldn't have read this far if you didn't at least suspect that your story is wrapped up in God's. So by now you may be asking the question, How do I actually discover my story and how it fits in the midst of God's story?

Though to this point we have majored on God's story, I have

offered hints along the way on how to connect it to your own. Now it is time to address more fully this practical outcome we've been aiming at since page one.

Remembering

Discovering the answer to your question requires, in part, remembering three things. The first thing we need to remember is the one plan of God's story. This is review—but none of us will find our place in the drama if the stage isn't set correctly for our scene. Remember this is God's plan: *To take one man (Abraham) and make from him one great nation (Israel) so that through it He might provide one great Savior (Jesus) who will extend God's grace and demonstrate God's glory to all creation.*

Keep this plan ever and always in view. Examine all of history, and your personal experience, through this lens of God's perspective. Whatever your story is to be, it will be intimately connected to this divine purpose. Your story is always going to be about advancing God's story. Ask yourself: How does God intend to use me to extend His grace and demonstrate His glory to all peoples?

The second thing we need to remember are the two fixed constants of God's story. Like the mariner's sextant which demands only two fixed points to allow him to accurately locate himself and chart his course, so we also need only to keep these two unchanging facts always in our view. These do not change. These two things are always true no matter where you find yourself in your journey or in God's story:

Everything about everything is about the glory of God.
Everything about everything is by the grace of God.

We each need to remember these two things about God's story. But now there is something we each must remember about our story. This is new. Make sure you don't miss the principle that is about to be set before you: *When you discover how God is uniquely committed to pouring His grace* into *your life, you will be well on your way to discovering how He intends to pour His grace* through *your life.*

Got it? Don't rush. Reread those lines. Marinate in this for a few moments. Let your soul steep in these thoughts.

Realize that this means there is some link between what has been going on in your life and what should be going on in your life. That is to say, God has been directing the affairs of your life all along. Connecting the dots of what He has been doing will help you begin to see how to connect the dots to what He yet wants to do in and through you. We will return to this principle shortly in order to make some sense out of what may until now have seemed like fragmented parts of your experience.

Inquiring

Finding your own story in God's story also requires asking yourself two questions. These questions may create some dis-comfort, but understand that they signal God's desire to extend His grace to you in a very personal way. He wants you to see what He sees—that He has loved you from before time, has been sovereign over the affairs of your life and wants to work through you to write a story that will be a part of His great plan. To that end, ask yourself this first question:

Am I unreservedly committed to God's glory?

Ponder that for a moment before you read on. Am I unre-servedly committed to God's glory?

Such a question may elicit several responses. You may im-mediately answer no! If that is the case, I'm sorry to hear it. I beg you to reconsider. But that is your prerogative. On the other hand, you may answer yes! If this is true, I rejoice with you. But I think reading on will help clarify the degree to which yes is an honest answer. While you may have answered yes or no, I'm guessing that most who read these lines are answering with something like this: "I'm all for God's glory. But am I unreserv-edly committed to it? I'm not sure. How would I know?"

I have gone through the pages of the New Testament looking for the kinds of cues that would signal utter, unreserved commitment to glorifying God. There are many, but let me bring forward just ten. Examine this series of statements drawn from the Scriptures and determine whether they are true of your life.

1. Absolutely nothing, inside or outside of me, enjoys the supreme place that belongs to God alone. (Rom. 1:21–23)
2. When suffering comes, I am at least as concerned with honoring God in the midst of the hardship as I am in getting out of it. (Rom. 8:17–18; 2 Cor. 4:17; Eph. 3:13; 1 Pet. 4:13–14)
3. When my rights conflict with another's needs, I choose the other person's needs over my rights. (1 Cor. 10:23–33)
4. I rely upon Christ's indwelling presence for what is necessary to live each moment for His purpose and honor. (Col. 1:27)
5. I make lifestyle choices based on my destiny as a child of God rather than upon my desires as an individual. (Eph. 4:1; 1 Thess. 2:12)
6. My life is driven by a sense of divine mission rather than personal maintenance. (Rom. 16:25–27; 2 Tim. 2:10; 1 Pet. 2:12)
7. When my will and God's will are at odds, I chose God's will. (Luke 22:42; Heb. 13:20–21)
8. My material and financial resources are devoted to fulfilling God's purposes to the extent that I live in active, continual trust that He will supply my daily needs. (Phil. 4:19)
9. My primary goal in life is not to succeed, achieve or "do," but to become more like Jesus Christ in my character and actions. (Rom. 8:29; 2 Cor. 3:18)

10. My reflex response to the events of life is one of gratitude. (1 Thess. 5:18; Heb. 13:15; Eph. 5:20)

If you've honestly examined yourself in the light of those questions, you may feel a bit overwhelmed. Please understand, this is not to determine whether you are perfect. I'm certainly not! You aren't either. Only God is. These questions should, however, help you determine whether the unabashed bent of your life is toward bringing as much glory to God as possible. When given the light to see that something in your life does not glorify God, do you change it? When given the light to see that something you might add to your life might help you glorify God more, do you make the adjustments necessary to add it to your life? Is every moment, every resource, all you are and own devoted to glorifying God?

We must ask and answer this question, because God has made no commitment to pour His grace into a life that is ultimately committed to something or someone other than Him and His glory. Thus, we need to settle this question first. Maybe you need to schedule a season of prayer to hear definitively from God on these matters. Any time so spent will be well worth the investment. But, when you are ready, move ahead to ask this second key question:

Am I unreservedly dependent upon God's grace?

Again, some may answer yes and others no! At the moment, I am concerned, however, for that majority of people who honestly ask, how would I know? If this includes you, I suggest that there are three primary ways God graces an individual's life.

The first is *saving grace*. The saving grace of God is where we each must begin. It is the news that God, in the Person of Jesus Christ, has stepped into our world. Jesus Christ lived the only perfect life ever lived, at every moment and in every circumstance fulfilling the perfect will of God and upholding all God's righteous demands. Having lived such a life, Jesus went to the cross, where He died, not for any sin of His own but for ours. Indeed, "the LORD has laid on him the iniquity of us all" (Isa. 53:6). There at the cross the Father poured out His judgment against our sin upon His sinless Son, who stood in our place.

When we turn from our sin and place our faith in Jesus Christ, an amazing transaction takes place. We discover that all our sin has been placed upon Christ (and thus we are free from its debt forever!) and that the righteousness of Christ is credited to our account in heaven. God declares us righteous. It is not that we are as yet actually righteous; but God, the great Judge, makes a judicial decision to declare us so and to set us before Himself as not just forgiven of our sin, but positively righteous! Not only this, but we are also regenerated to eternal life. We are given a new life. We are made to be children of God. We are set in a position of acceptance, love and honor. This is a gift. This is grace. This is saving grace.

Have you embraced the saving grace of God in Christ through repentant faith? Are you certain? It was for good reason that the apostle Paul exhorted those in the Corinthian church, "Examine yourselves to see whether you are in the faith; test yourselves" (2 Cor. 13:5). The saving grace of God in Christ is where we must each begin if our story is to be found a part of God's story. If you have embraced His saving grace, then you are ready to consider the next way that God graces our lives.

This is found in *sanctifying grace*. While saving grace declares us to be righteous, though we are as yet not righteous in practice, sanctifying grace follows it and is God's plan for making us actually righteous in thought, word, action and motive. He has declared us to be righteous—now God intends to make us what He has declared us to be. Sanctifying grace is God's plan to make us like Christ.

Paul told the Christians in Galatia that he would work and labor and pray over them "until Christ is formed in [them]" (Gal. 4:19). He told the believers in Philippi, "Your attitude should be the same as that of Christ Jesus" (Phil. 2:5). To the Christ-followers in the city of Colosse, he said that their salvation could be summed up in this way: "Christ in you, the hope of glory" (Col. 1:27). With the next sweep of his pen he told them, "We proclaim him, admonishing and teaching everyone with all wisdom so that we may present everyone perfect [mature] in Christ" (1:28).

Saving grace is an *event*. It happens in an instant. When we repent and place our faith in Christ, we are declared righteous by God and brought into relationship with God Himself as one of His children. But sanctifying grace is a *process*. It happens over a lifetime, as we cooperate with God's grace and see Christ's thoughts and words and deeds formed in our lives moment by moment. Those who truly embrace God's saving grace are plunged immediately into God's sanctifying grace. Saving grace, then sanctifying grace. This is always God's order.

It also helps to know that in His sanctifying grace God wastes nothing. He uses all our tragedies and triumphs, our honors and hardships toward the goal of making us more and more like His Son.

If you are to discover your place in God's plan, you must embrace God's saving grace and cooperate actively with Him in His sanctifying grace. The list of questions we looked at earlier will help you make an honest and probing evaluation of your progress toward Christlikeness. If you fail to embrace God's sanctifying grace, you will not discover how your story fits with His. But if you are doing so—not perfectly, but conscientiously and faithfully—then you are in a position to begin examining the third way that God graces our lives.

The third way God pours His grace into our lives is what I will call *signature grace*. Saving grace and sanctifying grace operate the same in all believers. The means by which each of us hears the one message of God's saving grace may vary—through a book, through a friend, perhaps through a sermon—but we all hear the same message of grace and are born again. And sanctifying grace may *look* different in how it is manifested in each of our lives—some at this moment are being refined through trials and others through triumphs—but all of us are being moved graciously along toward the same goal of Christlikeness. God's *signature* grace in your life, however, is unique to you.

Just what is God's signature grace? How might I identify His signature grace in my life? In just a moment I am going to give you some prompters that will help you identify this grace in your life. But to see it you will need to slip on a pair of lenses that will open your eyes to make out what you have perhaps been missing until now. Ready? Slip on the lenses of *sovereignty* and *providence*.

When you understand that God is *sovereign* over all things, you will begin to view your life differently. Not every detail of your life may have been God's will, but He is sovereign over your life, and in His *providence* He has been directing, allowing or redeeming what has happened to you. He has made His choices based upon His love for you and His commitment to His one plan.

God stands sovereignly over all His creation—including you. But in His providence God actively rules all He has created—including your life and all its details. It is by His providence that He has guided your life to this moment. Even when you walked in rebellion, God was setting the stage of your life so that your story might become part of His story. What has come into your life is a big part of what God wants to come of your life.

Do you believe this? Can you accept this? If so, you are ready to view your life from God's perspective. Consider these details in your own experience and how they point to the signature grace of God:

- Where you grew up and the kind of family you were born into

- The culture and language you were raised in
- The education you have/have not received (or are receiving)
- The temperament you were born with
- The natural abilities you have been graced with, both by birth and by experience
- The experiences of your life (both positive and negative)
- How you came to faith in Christ
- Early influences in your Christian life
- Sanctified hopes, dreams and desires that God has placed in your heart
- The spiritual gifts God has invested in you for building up His body and fulfilling His plan

A part of discovering your place in God's story is studying carefully the fingerprints of God upon your life. It is possible that it's a new experience for you to consider any of these as the fingerprints of God's grace. Yet they are just that. Apply much prayer to discerning God's grace in these things. Patiently wait for God's light of understanding in the area of His signature grace. Ask some trusted, godly friends to help you sort out some of the more difficult questions you may have in this area.

It may take time for clearer insight to arrive. You may need patience before you draw firm conclusions, but I believe you will find that when you discover how God is uniquely committed to pouring His grace *into* your life, you will be well on your way to discovering how He intends to pour His grace *through* your life.

So, I ask you again, Can you give an absolute, unqualified yes! to both of these searching questions? If so, then more than figuring out your story, you need to live out your story.

Huh?

What I mean is that if your answer to both questions is yes, then God is going to make certain your story is what it should be. God is more committed to His glory than you are. God is more committed to extending His grace to you than you are to receiving it.

If God's glory has captured your vision and His grace now owns your heart, you are unreservedly committed to the same thing that God is utterly devoted to—magnifying His glory and extending His grace to the peoples of the world through the gospel of Jesus Christ. If this is true, God will make your story a part of His story, and whether seemingly large or small, prominent or obscure, powerful or weak, your story will matter. Your life will make a contribution. You will be a part of God's plan. That is all any of us could ever ask, expect or hope. God will make it true.

You may be wondering, is that really true? Will that actually work? I mean, you are talking about the investment of the only life I will ever live!

An Encouraging Example

Allow me to show you how this worked out in the life of one man. His name is David. You will remember him from Act I, Scene 1. He was the king of Israel; at least that is how it eventually turned out. But it hadn't always seemed so certain that his accession to the throne would actually come to pass.

You may recall that the first king God set over Israel, Saul, had turned from God, and so God turned from him. Thus, God sent the prophet Samuel to anoint the next king over God's nation. Samuel was divinely directed to the household of Jesse. After all Jesse's sons had paraded before the prophet and still there was no signal that God's man had appeared, they finally brought the last son, a lowly shepherd boy. Heaven spoke. David was chosen. Samuel anointed him as the next king of Israel.

David's life was utterly changed—and, it seemed, not always for the better. Although David had been chosen by God, he wouldn't actively reign upon the throne for some years yet. The existing king, Saul, was jealous and began to seek David's death.

Somewhere during those tumultuous years of life on the run, David penned Psalm 57. The prescript to the psalm says David wrote it "when he had fled from Saul into the cave." David's heart was filled with questions about God's purposes, God's story, his personal story and what God was doing and allowing in his experience. In this prayer David wrote, "I cry out to God Most High, to God, who fulfills [his purpose] for me" (57:2). All was confusing. Nothing made sense. God's purpose appeared lost, cruel or indecipherable. So David cried out to God, clinging in faith to the promise that He is the One who "fulfills his purpose for me."

We have all been in that place when the events of life have turned so sour that the only hope we have left is that somehow God is still in charge and that He has not lost track of His plan. Prayers at such times are often made in desperation, just like David's was.

We find a similar expression coming from David in another of his psalms. At a different time and presumably under different circumstances, David wrote, "The Lord will fulfill his purpose for me" (138:8). Do you hear the change in tone? There seems to be a sense of confidence and restful faith, doesn't there?

Most of us seem to live out our days somewhere between the polar opposites of these two experiences. Some days I confidently affirm from my deepest heart that my life is in God's hand—that He is in charge, sovereignly orchestrating the events of my life toward the fulfillment of His good, pleasing and perfect will. Other days I am frantic and confused, clinging in desperate faith to the hope that God has not lost track of His purpose for my life, because I certainly can't see how anything going on in my experience can work out to His glory.

Have you been there too? If so, consider this final report about God's purpose and David's life. We have to race ahead approximately a thousand years from David's day. A millennium after David died, the apostle Paul almost casually reported,

"When David had served God's purpose in his own generation, he fell asleep [died]" (Acts 13:36).

It happened! Despite all the hardships, confusion, trials and tests—it actually came about! David's life "served God's purpose in his own generation"! And the good news is, so can yours. How? I'm going to leave you with one more word from David. Embrace and live by this, and God will eventually set up a sign over your life that will announce that you "served God's purpose in [your] own generation."

Here it is: "Trust in the LORD and do good . . . Delight yourself in the LORD and he will give you the desires of your heart" (Ps. 37:3–4).

- "Trust in the Lord"—that is unreservedly depending on His grace.
- "Do good"—that is going out to do the next thing you know God would have you do for the glory of His name.
- "Delight yourself in the Lord"—that is magnifying His glory and reveling in His grace.
- And "he will give you the desires of your heart"—that is God's assurance that your story will be a part of His.

Do this and you will have found your place in God's plan. End of story.

Writing My Story

Joyfully, intentionally and passionately writing your God-designed story is now within your grasp. If you have not already done so, take whatever time is necessary to patiently, prayerfully work through the two checklists presented earlier in this chapter. The lists relate to the two key questions regarding your personal commitment to experiencing God's grace and advancing His glory. More than anything else, answering these questions will position you to discover your place in God's plan.

Once you have answered these questions, let me suggest this exercise: Write out a covenant to God which specifically expresses your commitment to live by God's grace and for His glory. Take your time. Give yourself at least two weeks to finalize this covenant. Be realistic, yet stretch yourself forward in faith toward God's appointed goal.

Word the covenant in the form of a prayer to God. Be sure to give thanks for God's grace in your life and then commit to His glory through your life. Write a rough draft. Pray over it carefully for a number of days, making notes, corrections and changes as you sense God nudging you. Anchor your statements to specific Scriptures. Make certain that you clearly articulate your dependence upon God to fulfill your side of this commitment. Aim to express your commitment in timeless ways. Word it so that you can continue to pray this covenant decades from now, if God should grant you those years. Move no further until you sense God's release to finalize your prayer covenant with Him.

When you are ready, set aside a specific, protected time and place for an unhurried meeting with God. Type or write out the final draft of your covenant. On your knees (if possible) pray this covenant back to God. Then sign and date it before Him.

Your story is not found on the resulting piece of paper. Rather, it simply expresses your commitment, in dependence upon God, to invest all the assets (grace) that He has poured, is pouring and will pour into your life in His one plan of bringing glory to Himself. This is His story. You can trust Him to make it your story as well.

Now, rise in faith. Go forth. Live this out. Purpose to make this commitment the substance of your life, trusting that God will sovereignly and providentially make certain your story becomes an enduring contribution to His grand, global, eternal story.

Reviewing God's Story and Writing Your Story

Once more, review these key components of understanding God's story and discovering your own:

1. God's one great plan: To take one man
   (_____) and make from him one great nation (_____) so that through it He might
   provide one great Savior (_____) who will
   extend God's _____ and demonstrate
   God's _____ to all creation.

2. God's two fixed constants: Everything about everything
   is _____ the glory of God. Everything about
   everything is _____ the grace of God.

3. Ink with which to write your story: When you discover how God is uniquely committed to pouring His
   grace _____ your life, you will be well on your
   way to discovering how He intends to pour His grace
   _____ your life.

4. Three kinds of divine grace: _____
   grace, _____ grace and
   _____ grace.

Endnotes

ACKNOWLEDGEMENTS

1. Buck Hatch's course, The Progress of Redemption, and other teaching courses by him can be found at www. buckhatchlibrary.com.

INTRODUCTION: TELL ME A STORY

Epigraph. Robert Penn Warren in John Burt, ed., *The Collected Poems of Robert Penn Warren* (Baton Rouge: Louisiana State University, 1998), 267.
1. Merriam-Webster Online, http://www.merriam-webster. com/dictionary/story, accessed July 20, 2010. (Italics in quote are the author's emphasis.)
2. C.S. Lewis, *The Chronicles of Narnia* (New York: Harper, 2005), 767.

THE MASTER PLAN: TELL ME THE *REAL* STORY

Epigraph 1. John W. Gardner at www.quotationspage.com/ quote/3178.html, accessed July 6, 2009.
Epigraph 2. Norman Cousins, *Saturday Review*, April 15, 1978.
Epigraph 3. David C. McCullough in an address at Wesleyan University, June 3, 1984.
Epigraph 4. Cicero, *Pro Publio Sestio.*
1. André Maurios in Paul E. Billheimer, *Destined for the Throne* (Fort Washington, PA: CLC Publications, 1975), 19.
2. John Piper, *Seeing and Savoring Jesus Christ* (Wheaton: Crossway, 2004), 13–18.

3. James M. Hatch, *Progress of Redemption* (Columbia, SC: Columbia School of Biblical Education, 1984), 1:46–50.
4. Lewis, *The Four Loves* in Clyde Kilby, ed., *A Mind Awake: An Anthology of C.S. Lewis* (New York: Harcourt, Brace and World, 1968), 85.

THE STAGE SET: A SPURNED GRACE

Epigraph 1. Elie Wiesel, *The Gates of the Forest: A Novel* (New York: Avon Books, 1970), 10.
Epigraph 2. Lewis, *Christian Reflections* (Grand Rapids: Eerdmans, 1994), 105.
Epigraph 3. Joseph Ernest Renan, *The Life of Jesus* (New York: Carleton, 1864), 50.
Epigraph 4. Erich Auerbach, trans. Willard R. Trask, *Mimesis: The Representation of Reality in Western Literature* (Princeton: Princeton University Press, 1953), 15.
1. Buck Hatch notes this issue of proportionality in his book *Progress of Redemption*, 1:70.
2. I have expanded upon John J. Davis's connection between the opening words of Genesis 1:1 and the various "isms" of the world. See John J. Davis, *Paradise to Prison: Studies in Genesis* (Grand Rapids: Baker, 1975), 42.
3. A.W. Tozer, *The Pursuit of God* (Harrisburg, PA: Christian Publications, 1982), 81–82.

ACT I, SCENE 1: A PURSUING GRACE

1. Hatch calls the giving of God's Law the giving of a new culture to His people. See *Progress of Redemption*, 1:97–98.

ACT I, SCENE 2: A WEEPING GRACE

1. Wesley J. Duewel, *Ablaze for God* (Grand Rapids: Zondervan, 1989), 238.

Act I, Scene 3: A Faithful Grace

1. H.A. Ironside in Hatch, *Progress of Redemption*, 1:284.

2.   Boyd A. Luter and Barry C. Davis, *God Behind the Seen: Expositions of the Books of Ruth and Esther* (Grand Rapids: Baker, 1995).

INTERLUDE: A SILENT GRACE

1.   James Freedman at http://www.famousquotes.com show/1024995/, accessed September 14, 2009.
2.   Henri Nouwen in Jonathan Hunter, *Embracing Life Series* (Longwood, FL: Xulon, 2006), 177.
3.   J. Sidlow Baxter, *Explore the Book* (Grand Rapids: Zondervan, 1960), 5:11.
4.   St. John of the Cross in Richard F. Lovelace, *Dynamics of the Spiritual Life* (Downers Grove, IL: InterVarsity, 1979), 118.
5.   A.A. Attanasio in Xin-An Lu and Hong Wang, *A Manual of Guidelines, Quotations and Versatile Phrases for Basic Oral Communication* (Bloomington, IN: iUniverse, inc., 2003), 73.
6.   Luca Del Bo, Stella Forti, Umberto Ambrosetti, Serena Costanzo, Davide Mauro, Gregorio Ugazio, Berthold Langguth, Antonio Mancuso, "Tinnitus aurium in persons with normal hearing: 55 years later," *Otolaryngology—Head and Neck Surgery* September 2008 (vol. 139, no. 3, 391–94).
7.   E.M. Blaiklock, "Septuagint" in *The Zondervan Pictorial Encyclopedia of the Bible*, Merrill C. Tenney, gen. ed. (Grand Rapids: Zondervan, 1975, 1976), 5:342–43.
8.   Donald K. Campbell, *Daniel: God's Man in a Secular Society* (Grand Rapids: Discovery House, 1988), 162.
9.   H.C. Leupold, *Exposition of the Psalms* (Grand Rapids: Baker, 1969), 459.
10. Allan Harman, *Psalms: A Mentor Commentary* (Ross-shire: Christian Focus, 1998), 226.
11. Thomas Carlyle, *Sartor Resartus: The Life and Opinions of Herr Teufelsdrockh in Three Books* (Berkeley: University of California, 2000), 161.
12. Sir Robert Anderson, *The Silence of God* (Grand Rapids: Kregel, 1978), 1.

ACT II, SCENE 2: A SEEKING GRACE

1. Merriam-Webster Online, http://www.merriam-webster.com/dictionary/commission, accessed July 16, 2009.
2. A.B. Simpson in A.E. Thompson, *A.B. Simpson: His Life and Work* (Camp Hill, PA: Christian Publications, 1960), 111.

ACT III: A REALIZED GRACE

1. Gordon MacDonald, *Renewing Your Spiritual Passion* (Nashville: Thomas Nelson, 1986, 1989), 159.
2. The remainder of the chapter is adapted from my book *Embracing Authority* (Ross-shire, Scotland: Christian Focus, 2002). http://www.christianfocus.com/item/show/214/-/sr_1.
3. Archibald Thomas Robertson, *Word Pictures in the New Testament* (Grand Rapids: Baker, 1931), 4:357.
4. Millard J. Erickson, *Christian Theology* (Grand Rapids: Baker, 1983, 1984, 1985), 363.
5. Lewis, *The Chronicles of Narnia*, 767.

DISCOVERING YOUR STORY: A PERSONAL GRACE

Epigraph 1. William J. Bausch, *Storytelling: Imagination and Faith* (Mystic, CT: Twenty-third Publications, 1984), 171.
Epigraph 2. Malcolm Muggeridge, *Jesus: The Man Who Lives* (New York: Harper and Row, 1975), 47.
Epigraph 3. Lewis, *The Weight of Glory and Other Addresses* (New York: Macmillan Publishing Company, 1980), 92.

1. Elyse Schein and Paula Bernstein, *Identical Strangers* (New York: Random House 2007).

This book was produced by CLC Publications. We hope it has been life-changing and has given you a fresh experience of God through the work of the Holy Spirit. CLC Publications is an outreach of CLC Ministries International, a global literature mission with work in over fifty countries. If you would like to know more about us or are interested in opportunities to serve with a faith mission, we invite you to contact us at:

CLC Ministries International
PO Box 1449
Fort Washington, PA 19034

Phone: 215-542-1242
E-mail: orders@clcpublications.com
Website: www.clcpublications.com

DO YOU LOVE GOOD CHRISTIAN BOOKS?
Do you have a heart for worldwide missions?

You can receive a FREE subscription to
CLC's newsletter on global literature missions
Order by e-mail at:

clcworld@clcusa.org
Or fill in the coupon below and mail to:

PO Box 1449
Fort Washington, PA 19034

FREE _CLC WORLD_ SUBSCRIPTION!

Name: _____

Address:_____

_____

Phone: _____ E-mail:_____

READ THE REMARKABLE STORY OF
the founding of
CLC International

Leap of Faith

"Any who doubt that Elijah's God still lives ought to read of the money supplied when needed, the stores and houses provided, and the appearance of personnel in answer to prayer." —Moody Monthly

Is it possible that the printing press, the editor's desk, the Christian bookstore and the mail order department can glow with the fast-moving drama of an "Acts of the Apostles"?

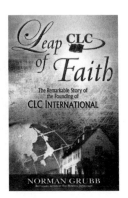

Find the answer as you are carried from two people in an upstairs bookroom to a worldwide chain of Christian bookcenters multiplied by nothing but a "shoestring" of faith and by committed, though unlikely, lives.

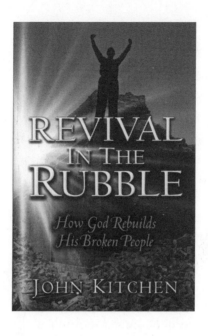

REVIVAL IN THE RUBBLE
John Kitchen

How God Rebuilds His Broken People

Can spiritual life and renewal ever be found in the midst of rubble and devastation? "Yes!" says John Kitchen. "When God wants to do a fresh, reviving work in His people, He finds a person and breaks his heart."

Do you read of great revivals in the past and find yourself asking God, "Why not here? Why not now? Why not me?" If so, pick up this book now.

Trade paper ISBN-13: 978-0-87508-873-0

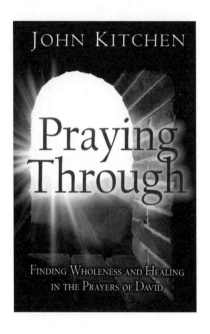

PRAYING THROUGH
John Kitchen

Betrayed? Humiliated? Lonely?
Feeling spiritually dry?

*How do you pray
when you're spiritually wounded?*

King David was betrayed, humiliated, felt lonely and experienced deep hurt and pain on every side. The psalms he wrote on those occasions are prayers that touch the heart of God. John Kitchen leads us on a healing journey through those prayers into a more intimate fellowship with our Father.

Trade paper ISBN-13: 978-0-87508-978-2

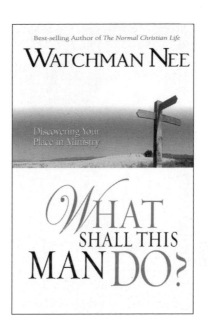

WHAT SHALL THIS MAN DO?
Watchman Nee

A fresh approach to the study of Christian service, its basic principles and motives, and the variety of means God uses in preparing men and women for it.

The great Chinese writer and preacher Watchman Nee was for many in the West a symbol of Christian steadfastness under the pressure of totalitarian government.

Trade paper ISBN-13: 978-0-87508-488-6

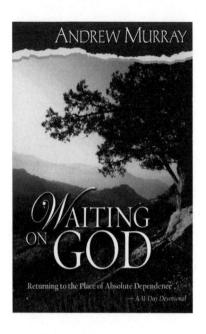

WAITING ON GOD
Andrew Murray

*"Has the life of God's people reached the
utmost limit of what God is willing to do for them?
Surely not!"*

With this bold statement, Andrew Murray challenges
believers to practice the art of waiting only on God. In thirty-
one chapters, arranged as readings for each day of the month,
Murray leads us in the school of waiting—of being silent before
God in complete trust and dependence.

Invest thirty-one days with Murray in waiting upon God—
the results will be more than you could ask for.

Trade paper ISBN-13: 978-0-87508-854-9